RESAVAGER
VOLUME 1

BY

FRONTIER DISCIPLE

RESAVAGER
VOLUME 1

Published by RESAVAGER Media

RESAVAGER.COM

Table of Contents

Preface to the First Volume

RESAVAGER is the name of the substack I started in 2020 as a solution to a problem I faced on twatter. Saying what you wanted to say was a fast track to being banned and at the same time, the platform did not support long form writing. The first essays published on RESAVAGER were very much free form. There was no attempt to polish or proofread them. I just wanted to say what I wanted to say. This first volume represents my writing from the first year and half of RESAVAGER. These essays while not necessarily my complete thought, show the beginnings of how it developed.

Not every essay made it. I only included essays that are worth your time and quality being called "evergreen." You will find in the first section many references to Pagan Gods like Odin and Mars not so much because I subscribe to their faith (something impossible in our time as the rites have been lost to time), but that they offer important lessons for us today. Heracles, the spiritual mascot of RESAVAGER, is prominent in these first essays. He is criminally underrated as a figure worth studying to which I blame Hollywood for their terrible depictions of the Grek hero. Heracles must be made the symbol of our future. He was a complicated man who made terrible mistakes during his lifetime but resolved to be absolved of his sins before The Gods.

RESAVAGER: Vol 1 will cover a variety of topics that I've narrowed down to six main categories. The first of which is the WISDOM to be gained from the Old Gods. Learning this wisdom is vital to our time because our enemies have hidden the reality nature and the true way of the world whereas our ancestors who worshipped these Gods did so because they taught them how to survive and thrive in nature. As a subset of this category, we will discuss the subject of devotion — a feeling lost to the modern world. Religions seem to have lost all power before the new faith of leftism. Where is the fanaticism? The fervor towards life?

Extreme belief and devotion will carry a man through the most vicious of hells. As Nietzsche said, "he who has a why can endure almost any how." There are aspects of our life that exist as mere routine or even hobby when they should be made sacred and ritualized so that our bloodline never forgets their importance. The second category deals squarely with Americans and builds the foundation for my understanding of what an American is, something still debated today. Americans ARE a race. This race does not include the recent migrants or anyone that claims some hyphenated "identity."

Americans must endure two decades worth of psychological warfare by the kingdom of darkness — which wears our nation as a skin suit — before they are sent out to be a cow to be milked by their masters. They're told all through their impressionable years that they should be ashamed of their ancestors. That their race was never great. They are not their own people, nor do they have any culture. All of this while living in the empire built by their forefathers, speaking the language of their forefathers. We are a people severed from their ancestral history and my Great Work is to reforge this thread.

The next two categories are small and deal with topics I don't really write about anymore but are important to the overall message none the less. The first deals with rhetoric aimed to save what you consider salvageable frens on the left. This is a worthy goal as half of our race have been seduced by the enemy and not all of them are beyond saving. The idea of spending by your time trying to un-mindfuck the leftist is not an effective strategy in the long run. You are better off first winning battles and when you establish yourself as a winner, they will flock to your side as evidenced by the barbarian tribes in the Second Punic War. This is human nature.

After this, there is a section on fitness. Working to improve the fitness of our race is a grand goal. Nietzsche tells us that the body must be convinced first. It's well known that any man who takes seriously his physicality will be forced to leave the left and move towards a position conducive to nature. It's a portal to our side. I've trained consistently for over fifteen years now. It's part of my life that will never go away. It's my hope that all who find our path share this same passion for fitness.

The fifth section will deal primarily with war. Heraclitus tells us that "War is the father and king of all." There can be no denying that war is the ultimate aim of man. It's what he was born for. Now not every war is what you want it to be, but if you can frame it as such, you will go on the warpath. It's my aim to have every American waking up ready to go to war. In this life, you have to fight.

This leads to last category: the barbarian and barbarism. In my own journey, I came to the conclusion that the way of nature is barbaric. There is no avoiding it. No sticking to the "humanist" path of our enemies. Barbarism is, of course, the natural state of man and you may forget it at your own peril. The other reason for choosing this name is that once you embrace the values necessary to survive and thrive in nature, you will be seen only as a barbarian by your enemies.

This will be the first of yearly volumes of RESAVAGER. Many have asked me to put these essays in print and so I have. These essays are remastered and made evergreen. I hope you enjoy.

PART I:

DEVOTION

1.
Wisdom of the Old Gods

Mankind is a subverted species. Until the emergence of Christianity, men worshipped Gods and religions designed to inspire strength and courage among their ranks. The Old Gods were strong and powerful because men needed strength and power to survive in the wilderness.

Christianity, however, came out of the peak of the Roman Empire. The technology at the time was so advanced that it took hundreds of years after the fall to recreate and surpass the Romans. It's no coincidence Christianity sprang from the Romans. Life was easier there than any other place at the time. It was a religion of slaves. Born from what Nietzsche called slave morality.

Most Christians today can be found on the right. The modern left holds Christians in poor regard because of this but their values are copied straight from Judeo-Christian values. They have more in common than they realize. This is not attack on the Christian Right. I hope a new vitalist denomination of Christianity comes forth in the spirit of their Crusader ancestors.

The biggest problem with leftism is that they continue the same life-denying virtues of Christianity but without the promise of salvation upon death. Leftism, Marxism, Bolshevism — whatever you want to call it — is the natural evolution of Christianity. The religion remains the same, only the gods they worship have changed. Instead of Jesus and the One God, it has become scientism and social justice. But these people aren't virtuous in the way the Christian tries to be virtuous.

They're devoid of power and vitality. Instead, they're immersed in degeneracy and decadence. They live in defiance of natural law. How long nature will allow this to go on is yet to be seen. The Christian suffers so that he may find paradise in heaven. But what does the leftist suffer for? Moral superiority and comfort?

The leftist — a mere tool of the elite — believes himself morally superior and on the "right side of history." The arrogance, amirite? History hasn't been written yet. The leftist is life-denying. It's better to be safe than sorry. He's terminally committed to the doctrine of equality even as it actively undermines his own vitality and happiness. Why? To feel himself morally superior.

The leftist will reject his own vitality and happiness. He will welcome policies that will keep him wretched and poor, just so he can take the high ground. So, he can be an "ally." This on a mass scale is simply racial suicide. The cleansing fire won't be kind to them.

It's best to understand the modern left like those still plugged into the matrix. Most will never be unplugged. They will remain ignorant. Hell, they will fight to save the same system that enslaves them. You can hate them, but it's not their fault. Most of the world is brainwashed and controlled by a hidden elite. There's no hope of victory against leftism in outright warfare. You must become a guerrilla fighter.

2.

In the Old Pagan Gods, you can find the path back to nature. Once you can grasp real nature and man's place in nature, you increase your odds of victory in the great game. The Old Gods are the true means of salvation. Salvation from what? From eternal damnation? From the "wrong side of history?" No, they're salvation from modern slavery and slave morality.

Looking to the Old Gods gives you the chance to return to nature and become who you were meant to be. I'm not suggesting you start worshipping the Old Gods, simply learn about their religions, their stories, and the wisdom they left behind. The modern liberal just sees these religious tales as fantasy and finds no greater meaning in them. You must search for meaning as Odin did when he hung from the world tree.

Take Heracles for example. The meaning of his 12 Labors is not that he is ridiculously strong and powerful(no doubt the son of Zeus), for the story of Heracles is less about strength, and more about resilience and virtue. We have made Heracles a boring hero — like Superman — when he's far more than some comic book hero.

What you don't learn about Heracles is that he was offered the choice between an easy life of vice or a hard life of virtue. After thinking for a long time about the decision, he chose the life of virtue. Many don't know that he only took on the 12 Labors as an act of redemption. Hera had poisoned his mind and in a fit of wild rage, he killed his wife and children.

Did you also know that the 12 Labors were originally 10? King Eurystheus, whom he was serving to atone for his sins, cheated him out of two of the labors and made him do two more. Many of his labors had him conquering chthonic monsters and making the world safe for mankind.

His third labor required him to capture the Ceryneian hind. He injured the beast in the process, angering the Goddess Artemis, but he defied even The Gods to complete these labors. This act was more than redemption. It showed devotion and the power of his will. It is why we still remember the name Heracles. His labors were his Great Work, his mark on the world.

Heracles is a fine example for men seeking greatness. It's not his strength and power that you get from his story, but his devotion and will to power. He kept moving forward no matter what hardship was thrown upon him. He repented for any sin he made along the way, even submitting himself to slavery for a wrongful death by his own short temper.

3.

Was Odin the father of the Aesir or was he a man who became a God?

Odin is steeped in mystery. He's known by over thirty names. His stories talk about how he takes many forms to deceive people. He hung himself from the world tree to receive the knowledge of the runes. A sacrifice as he says, from himself to himself.

Through this act, he learns of Ragnarok — the Twilight of The Gods where he is swallowed up by the great wolf. He sees Thor's battle with the world snake and the beginning of the next age. An age without the Aesir. He's called by the Norse the Allfather, but there's another rumor about Odin less known.

His act of sacrifice. Removing his eye for wisdom. Stabbing himself with a spear and hanging from the world tree to learn the secrets of the runes was not just sacrifice for knowledge, but his own ascension from man to God. Some believe Odin was once a great king who became a God.

I enjoy this idea because it should be the goal of every man to become a God. Whether or not there are or aren't Gods isn't the point. To get your name remembered throughout time — that is becoming a God. It's leaving a mark on the world so big you will never be forgotten.

Learn the wisdom of the old Gods. Learn what they're really about. Strength and power and vitality. You should — as Nietzsche implores you — say yes to life. Be life-affirming. We don't know what lies beyond. It's best now to live the greatest life you can and establish your legend for the coming ages.

4.
MARS ULTOR

This is a Mars Ultor — Mars the Avenger — Respecter account. Nietzsche diagnosed what we already know today, that "God is dead." Now among the Christian true believers, the faith is strong. But the Christians are disprivileged in the West. If you're Christian, don't hate Nietzsche for saying this. He was only diagnosing a problem we see clearly today. In his time, it was only in its infancy. Bronze Age Pervert said on his show, Caribbean Rhythms, that the solution to this gay age we live in is religion, so if you're Christian you must look to create a new manly denomination to retake power.

Christian or not, learning about the Pagan Gods is valuable. There are lessons learned by our ancestors that get passed down through culture, myths, and religion. The Roman Gods get the bad rap of being ripped off from their Greek counterparts, but this may be just more liberal mocking of religion. There were many Roman Gods. You could say the Romans saw nature as being moved by divine power. There was even a God of the dung heap. The nature of the God Mars is primordial to the Roman culture.

Mars is the Roman counterpart to the Greek god Ares. Ares was loathed by the Greeks. He represented the ugliness of war, the wrath and bloodlust of the warrior. His sons — who fought at his side during battle — were called fear and panic. Mars in his inception into Roman culture was different. He wasn't the terrible and shameful God Ares was to the Greeks. Hell, the Roman origin story puts the Roman God of War as the father of Romulus and Remus, the founders of Rome.

The meaning of the name Mars is MARTIAL which means the character suggested of a warrior. Where Ares was the pure bloodlust of the warrior, Mars was also an agricultural guardian to the Romans. He was the epitome of the Roman phrase, "If you want peace, prepare for war." Mars is associated with marital savagery and the wild woodlands. His origins were as both of a thunderer like Zeus or Thor and a God of the wild. He existed beyond the boundaries of men, guarding the perimeter. Later on, other Gods took over His roles of the storm and fertility.

The symbol of Mars is the spear and shield, which you also see in the symbol we use to designate the symbol of man in modern culture. He's seen more as a defender and protector of men, unlike his Greek counterpart who is the bloodlust of battle. Mars is manliness. He comes into being when you train and prepare for war. He is the savagery of battle. Mars holds off nature to protect the people and their crops. The animals associated with Mars are the woodpecker, the wolf, and the bear.

One of the greatest rituals done to Mars was called devotio, from which we get the word devotion. This ritual is performed by a Roman General who wants to ensure his victory by sacrificing not only the lives of the enemy but his own. He would perform the sacred rites of devotion and then, make sure he was on the frontlines to meet his end in the battle. The General sacrificing his life for his army's victory, how does this make you feel? Honor and glory are more important than just living long in the eyes of great men. If you're a man after greatness, power, and glory, you should pay your respect to Mars. Be warned, Mars is not a God you can just pray to. You may gain his favor through action only.

SI VIS PACEM, PARA BELLUM

5.
THE DEVOTION OF HERACLES

The story of Heracles has captivated me in this degenerate age. So many men are removed from nature and one of the few surviving stories about natural law, along with what it means to be a man, can be found in Ancient Greek mythology. *The Iliad*_and *The Odyssey* are must-reads, as well as, The 12 Labors of Heracles.

This age requires strong men of devotion and intolerance. There is no better way to introduce your friends to natural law than the story of Heracles. No, not the Hollywood Hercules, the actual Heracles.

Heracles wasn't the dumb, lovable guy from the Disney movie or even Kevin Sorbo. Heracles for the Greeks was their most famous hero. He was a hunter and warrior, a monster slayer. Heracles set out into the fog of war and made the world safe for mankind by conquering the ancient monsters. He founded sea routes and slew beasts.

His Labors weren't done out of goodwill but for redemption. Heracles — out of a drunken rage or the influence of Hera — killed his own wife and children. With the guidance of the Oracle at Delphi to appease the Gods for his crime, he was made to serve an unworthy king who issued him the 12 Labors.

Everyone knows about his 12 Labors, but fewer still could name them all. The easy ones would be the Nemean Lion, the Hydra, and Cerberus, but how many talk about his Third Labor — the Cerynitian Hind? The hind was sacred to the Goddess Artemis. He spent a year tracking the beast. He could not harm it, for the hind was sacred to Artemis. To hurt it, would incur Her wrath.

After having worn down the beast, Heracles wounded the hind with an arrow. This allowed him to finally — after an entire year — catch the hind. He put the hind over his shoulder and headed back to Mycenae to complete the labor. Once he reaches Arcadia, however, he is confronted by Artemis and her brother, Apollo. The Goddess was angered and wanted the hind returned to her.

Heracles refused. Yes, that's RIGHT. Heracles refused the Goddess. This act is very powerful. Heracles' defiance of the Goddess is something not talked about. To go against The Gods is blasphemous, it's taboo. It's hard to understand the significance of this moment because we no longer believe in The Gods. Perhaps, you can compare it to going against the mob today. The desire to fit in, and conform, with your social group is high. It's not easy to go against a group that will ostracize you.

He is choosing to go against The Gods to complete his Labors. Heracles said he wounded the hind out of necessity. Eurystheus wanted the hind captured and he would bring him the hind. If she wants to be angry at someone, be angry at the King who ordered the Labor done.

Lucky for Heracles, Artemis accepted this response. She healed the hind and allowed Heracles to go on his way. His defiance was an act of intolerant devotion to his purpose. Heracles would even go against the Gods of Olympus to complete his Labors. His brute manliness wouldn't be intimidated by Artemis. This is something as a man you must internalize. Your purpose, your Great Work, is primary, over all other things.

Heracles set out for redemption. He wanted to set things right between him and The Gods after the brutal killing of his family. These Labors would make him remembered, they would give him everlasting fame. But they also came with great pain and sacrifice. It took him a decade to complete the 12 Labors. That my friends is devotion.

The men of our time always choose the easy way. The way of Netflix, the way of the video game, and the cell phone. It's unlikely that any man of this time can channel the absolute, intolerant devotion required to complete these Labors today. This you must dwell on because as modern men, we have no doubt angered The Gods with disgusting blasphemies.

The way we live now is against natural law. It cannot be maintained. A more savage people — who haven't sacrificed their virile fighting power — will eventually conquer us if we don't correct course. It's a matter of time, and now is the best time to seek redemption. You must repent for your part in modernity. You must undertake great labors, forge Great Works, and establish noble bloodlines. You must make sure your name and bloodline are remembered.

Greatness, power, and glory — those are your goals, your intolerant devotion to purpose.

6.
THE ADVENTURES AND BRUTALITY OF YOUNG HERACLES

Another title of this might be Alceides Rising. Most don't know that Heracles wasn't born Heracles. His birth name was Alceides. He only took on the name by request of the oracle — to stave off the rage of Hera.

It was by Hera's will that Alceides was sent into a wild madness that killed his wife and children. By modern morality, we wouldn't hold Alceides responsible for his tragedy as they say about parents who leave their kids in a car on a hot summer day, he suffered enough. But this wasn't enough for the Ancient Greeks and The Gods. The Oracle at Delphi said that to atone himself for this tragedy, he had to serve King Eurystheus for ten years and complete ten labors.

Heracles wasn't the goody-two-shoes hero we get from Hollywood. He was a man like any one of us, culpable of making mistakes. The difference would be that he chose the life of virtue over the life of comfort. There's an old tale about Alceides, before he became Heracles, whereas a young man he wandered into the forest and was confronted by two women who represented the crossroads of his life. The first woman was Vice. She offered a life of comfort and pleasure. The second woman was Virtue, and she offered a life of hardship and honor. After thinking on it for some time, he chose virtue.

Before he was Heracles, he was Alceides, but make no mistake he still had the blood of Zeus surging through his veins. The beginning of Heracles didn't start with the violent killing of his family. By then, he was already a famous warrior and killer.

Being the stepson of a king, Alceides was taught chariot driving, wrestling, archery, fencing, and lyre-playing. The latter, however, didn't end well. The man teaching Alceides struck him and an angry Alceides took his lyre killed his teacher with it. They tried to charge Alceides with murder, but Alceides stated a law which we would be familiar with. Self-defense. He had not initiated the violence; he was only defending himself.

His stepdad — fearing something like this happening again — sent him to manage his herds. This is where he grew up to be the strong and massive hero, we remember him as. It was said just looking at him was enough to know he was the son of Zeus.

Sometime later, he went on a hunt to kill a lion that was attacking both his and Thespios(the king of Thespiae) herds. The hunt lasted fifty days. He was given one of Thespios' fifty daughters to be entertained by. Little did he know, the old king wanted each of his daughters to get the seed of Alceides so he had a different daughter lay with him each night.

But wait, there's more! The step father of Alceides was the king of Thebes. Some years before Alceides, the Minyan King was mortally wounded by a member of the Theban royal family. His son came to Thebes to avenge his death, and after defeating the Thebans, made a treaty with them. The Thebans were made to give the Minyans a hundred cattle every year for twenty years.

Alceides didn't think much of the arrangement, however, for when the heralds came to collect the cattle, he subjected them to shameful mutilation. He cut from them their ears, noses, and hands of which he fastened to cords that he put him around their necks. Alceides told them to take those back as tribute to the Minyan king Erginos. This of course, led to another war between the Thebans and Minyans.

Alceides took command of the Thebans, wearing armor from Athena, killed Erginos, and sent the Minyans away in flight. In the aftermath, a new treaty was made. This time it would be the Minyans paying tribute, but at a rate of two hundred cattle a year for forty years. Double the terms they had imposed on the Thebens. That's RIGHT. Thats what you get! Do NOT lose wars. It was this battle where Alceides would be awarded the woman who would become his wife and she would bear him three sons.

It's worth mentioning that the Greeks knew these stories and still celebrated Heracles as their most famous hero. How does this make the leftists feel? The Ancient Greeks and all ancient peoples understood nature for what it was: barbaric. No goody-two-shoes would survive in the natural world. If you think you can get on the list of great men in history and not be a killer, you've got another thing coming.

I encourage you to take another look at Heracles. This time from what the Greeks actually wrote about him. What I talked about here comes from Apollodorus. Reading the Ancient Greeks will show you how men in nature really acted. They cared about honor and shame on a level modern leftists couldn't comprehend. Justice also had a different meaning. I'm certain almost all Greeks would have celebrated the Minyans' punishment after their battle with the Thebans. The great men of history are almost always bad men as Lord Acton said. We don't remember good guys. We remember conquerors.

7.
WHO WILL BE THE NEW HERACLES?

The Greek hero Heracles has become a favorite of mine in recent years. His story used to bore me before I read the actual source material. He was the Disneyfied Superman(boring) of the Greek demigods. But if you read Apollodorus, you realize he was nothing of the sort.

The heroes of our time are watered down. Made to be good and wholesome champions of liberal democracy, which is fitting for a society that's forgotten its place in nature. It's not that nature doesn't matter anymore, it's that in our great hubris, we think we've mastered nature. And you see it in the rhetoric. Despite whatever technological advancements we've made, we still exist within the confines of nature.

We remember Heracles as the first hero. He set out into nature, a dark and dangerous world full of chthonic monsters that terrorized the common folk. We remember Heracles because he tamed the world for mankind by conquering these monsters.

His reasons weren't purely noble. He was a man seeking redemption in the eyes of Gods and men. Heracles completed his Twelve Labors to atone for killing his wife and children. Regardless, he was spurred into action by Nemesis. Nemesis to us moderns means like an adversary, but to the Greeks, Nemesis meant to give what is due.

The Greek story of Heracles seems impossible in modern times. There are no more monsters, right? The two aren't as separated as you'd think. We just have different monsters. Imagine some dystopian America — basically the same America we live in now — that gave birth to a new, modern Heracles.

Now imagine this new Heracles, on the run from the law, seeking guidance from some Native American shaman on how he can redeem himself before The Gods. He's made to serve some billionaire for ten years and by doing so, he will be redeemed and made into a God.

This billionaire has scores to settle and uses Heracles as his battle axe. Fast forward to breaking news, straight from a CNN helicopter recording an ongoing terrorist attack on Amazog

Headquarters. Blurry pictures are then shown of the suspect. A hulking man wearing a lion's pelt, battle armor, and multicam BDUs is shown dual-wielding machine guns.

The reporter then starts talking about Jeff Bezos trying to escape from a helicopter on the roof. Authorities are unable to get to the scene due to a coordinated trucker strike blocking the roadways. As the helicopter starts to lift off, its tail is shot to hell by Heracles, and it wrecks on the landing pad.

Our new Heracles pulls an injured Bezos from the burning helicopter and [redacted] him live on TV. Seeing the news helicopter, Heracles fires on CNN next forcing the helicopter to retreat from the horrific scene.

Every institution in America would be mobilized against Heracles. Conservatives would talk about how it was Bezos' American right to build up his wealth like he did. He worked hard for it. Heracles was a psychopath. They'd even start the rumors that Heracles was a White supremacist who murdered his own family.

Liberals will have the talking points about how yes, no one should be as rich as Bezos but the man donated so much money to minorities and was the first to recognize the power of diversity, having mandated it in all Whole Foods stores. They would parrot the talking point of how Heracles is a Neo-Nazi and authorities found a copy of *Mein Kampf* in his home.

Would Heracles get around to finishing the labors asked of him? Or would the wide-sweeping propaganda machine brainwash enough people to undermine and overpower the Son of Zeus? Perhaps, his billionaire financier would sow the seeds of chaos into the nation to stop the institutions from thwarting the new Heracles?

Would Heracles be dissuaded from continuing his labors in such a world or would he carry it out undaunted? After his Twelve Labors, new Heracles stands upon the heaping ruins of the old United States with machine gun in hand and an American flag flying in the background. He ushers in a new age for the country where the people aren't oppressed by stifling bureaucracies and corrupt institutions.

He's made the world safe for mankind again. No longer are the people made sickly and mentally ill by their evil overlords looking to milk them for everything they're worth. Life may have been made harder, but infinitely more fulfilling. For a man to do this, he would have to shut out the corporate brainwashing of the media. He would have to understand it was either victory or death. New Heracles would have to have been spurred by powerful thumos. The dystopian monsters of our age were an affront to his honor before The Gods.

To make this heroic tale lame, technology has dwarfed the strength of heroes. How long till the government just drone strikes new Heracles in the middle of one of his labors? Would other nations capitalize on the chaos? What would a new Heracles have to be like in modern times to succeed?

The world is always changing. Even today where nothing seems to happen, you can see world powers maneuvering against one another. Only leftists think history has ended. Only modern Americans believe that bullshit. No one can say what tomorrow will hold. What we do know is no empire sticks around forever. The age of heroes is far from over. This is why you must still build yourself. Embrace the Barbaric Vitalism of our ancestors. Become strong and powerful.

8.
PAGAN DEVOTION

I grew up in a Christian family, but never really believed — hell, I identified not so much as an atheist, but agnostic. Something, of course, created this world. My views have changed in the past couple of years, but not because I found Jesus or anything to that effect.

RESAVAGER speaks a lot about devotion because devotion — as a concept — is powerful. Many treat activities like fitness and nutrition as hobbies that you kind of follow and that's fine. But for me, the act of training itself is devotion, devotion to your highest self.

Maybe it's age, maybe it's the chaos that is this degenerate age, but devotion is something this world needs. Most people worship science just as dogmatically as any Christian or Muslim worships their religion. The problem is these worshippers of science are spiritually bankrupt. They look at the men and religions of the past as backward and bigoted. These people will look at America a couple hundred years ago and only see slavery, not the grit the first Americans had to have to survive on the frontier.

Devotion is not optional but required if you want to be anyone of worth. The new age we're living in is like a greasy used car salesman. The mainstream culture wants you to believe in unnatural ideologies like egalitarianism and globalism. What they don't understand or realize is there is a reason why our ancestors acted as they did and it's not because they were uneducated.

The new age wants you to believe it's ok — no, it's the ideal — to be fat, ugly, and weak, to even go so far as making up your own gender. Nor should you have to deal with any of the negative connotations of those things. They want you to have the free reign of mediocrity. Eat what you want, and don't worry about your health or how you look — real men don't care about how they look. Just make sure you go to college, vote democrat, and stick it to the evil bible thumping republicans.

There are always consequences to the actions you take. If you spend much of your life being fat and unhealthy, you're going to be vulnerable to a renegade Chinese virus. The older I get, the more I see the importance of religion and being a man of devotion. You can approach your life with the consumerist mindset of this culture, hell, you can even have some productive hobbies like lifting and martial arts. You can get obsessed with self-creation, but devotion — devotion is on another level entirely.

Choosing to live like the consequences don't matter leads down a dark, ugly road. Even the zealots and fanatics of degenerate culture don't want it. They've either given up or haven't found a way out of hell. If you choose ugly, you will become ugly. Give people the easy path and they'll choose it nine times out of ten. It's the devoted man who chooses the hard road because he sees beyond the first-order consequences of his actions. This man of principle will endure hardship to obtain greatness. The degenerate man will choose easiness to obtain temporary comfort. He doesn't see past his immediate desires. This is the reason I've become religious in my advanced age.

Left to their own devices, men become retarded. Just look at 2020 America. 330 million people doing what they want, living the consumerist lifestyle while leading the world in obesity and compromised immune systems. If that wasn't enough, you have a people who think there are more than two genders and to be an inclusive society you must have open borders, and lower standards so women and minorities can qualify for positions held by American men, while telling those men they're toxic for...being who they are.

I'm certain the majority who read this won't find any fault with those ideologies and absurdities. They'll take great offense to me. Know that if you choose to be a fat slob, you'll be fragile like a fat slob. This is why men need religion. They must feel a deep devotion to an idea, a goal, a Great Work.

9.
MY PAGAN DEVOTION

I can't follow Christianity. The religion has been co-opted by the progressive virus. Beyond that, I can't bring myself to worship a weak God. Sorry to the Christians reading this. I don't consider you on the wrong path, it's just not the path for me. I'm more of a Pagan. I don't believe so much in the existence of The Gods, but rather in the wisdom of their mythology.

The Gods, as well as, great men, should be held to the highest regard and inspiration. I'll touch on two Gods that inspire me today. In Ancient Rome, the Romans built statues of great men and Gods to be inspired by them. Through that inspiration, you saw a Roman Republic that was powerful because its people believed that the demonstration of will through labor was high virtue. That laziness was cowardice. The Romans also believed in the redemption of lost honor, unlike modern cancel culture where you say the wrong thing and you're ruined. To them, reclaiming your honor was like how we, as Americans, love to see the underdog overcome and win. The Roman legion who defeated Hannibal in Africa were the survivors of the massacre at Cannae. They chose to redeem their honor by serving under Scipio Africanus with no pay. That's how important their honor was to them. The Romans are good examples for Pagans.

Heracles is another. Heracles to the Greeks was the hero who made the world safe for mankind by slaying monsters and mapping sea routes. There's no telling how many women he conquered, but his descendants, called the Dorians, eventually set up many city-states, the most famous one we know as Sparta.

His Twelve Labors were originally ten, but his nemesis, King Eurystheus, claimed he cheated on two of them and refused to count them. Hercules devoted ten years to completing his labors, all to seek redemption from The Gods for his drunken (or poisoned-crazed) killing of his wife and children.

Heracles was far from the boring, good-guy hero we're told he is. He killed, he fucked, he conquered. You know about his famous labors — slaying the Nemean Lion, defeating the Hydra, or wrestling Cerberus, but my favorite labor is Cerynitian hind. It is during this labor that he's confronted by The Gods for wounding the sacred hind and he does what most, if not all of us, would not: he refuses to return the hind, to supplicate to The Gods. He pleaded necessity and told them if they wanted to blame anyone, blame Eurystheus for ordering the labor. Tell me, would you have the courage to stand against The Gods?

During his journeys, Heracles shows he's not just a boring hero like Superman. He is forced to show his wits and devotion to his cause. Strong as he may have been, his resilience was stronger. Heracles was a man who understood what it meant to become a great man. His labors were his great work, and he shall always be remembered because of them.

Thor is another God RESAVAGER holds in high honor. Thor represents the warrior archetype. He represents brute manliness, and, unlike the Christian god, you can't pray to him — you can only join his gang. Thor is the red blood pulsing through your veins when you're defending the perimeter of your tribe, pushing a heavy weight over your head, or practicing a martial art.

Where Heracles for us represents strength and is the patron of gymnasiums, Thor is joy of combat and contest. He exists to protect mankind. While Heracles seeks out greatness and power, Thor is in the fray, defending mankind from chaos. Both of these Gods must be channeled into the man of devotion.

Ours is the way of power, winning, and freedom.

10.
DEVOTION TO GREATNESS, POWER, AND GLORY

Devotion to purpose, devotion to your Great Work, this is underrated quality in modern men. I know when you hear the word "devotion," you think of religious men which may rub you wrong way in this age of science. I use the word devotion however, by design. Mankind — and you as man — needs devotion.

Strongly devoted, religious men have done far more for mankind than the dweeb scientific types. This does not mean I believe you should find your nearest church and convert to Christianity or Islam. This means only that you must become a man of devotion to some higher cause beyond yourself. Ernst Jünger said of the men marching off to fight in WWI that they were men looking for "greatness, power, and glory." How many men dwell on such things today? Your average modern man is just looking for good job and a female who will give him the time of day.

You must find your own religion, you must worship Gods that represent greatness, power, and glory in your own mind. I don't ask you to abandon science and modernity. There is much value in science. It's the devotees of scientism, the iNtElLeCtuAls that you must avoid and shun like the plague. These zealots believe themselves on the side of science and experts, but they don't have the slightest comprehension of nature or even human nature. They see scientists as modern-day priests — pure and Godly — without recognizing that they're just men. A scientist during the pandemic is FINALLY feeling important, FINALLY feeling someone is listening to him. Do you not think that will influence him? By the same token, do you think the scientist is incorruptible because he's a devotee to science? A scientist is just as corruptible as a politician. To believe differently is to carry great naivety.

Religion and devotion is worth far more than the worship of some God. It's more the devotion to self, to some higher reason beyond your terrestrial needs. It's a way of living focused on self-creation and high vision. It's taking the solar path.

The terrestrial is of the earth. It's your basic needs to feel safe, secure, and loved. For most men, it's just having a good job and a family. But if you choose only to seek the terrestrial, that of the earth, you will be greatly unfulfilled. I believe most modern depression stems from seeking only the terrestrial existence.

You must be a man of high vision on the solar path to find fulfillment in life. The pursuit of the Great Work, of greatness, power, and glory, is what will bring you the "good life." Too many men are stuck in the weeds, when they should be looking to the sky. We all know the saying, "It's better to shoot for the stars and fail, than the sky and succeed."

It's no mistake that most religions believe their Gods come from the sky, the heavens. Christianity believes heaven is above us. Mount Olympus is a massive mountain in the heavens. Thor is a god of the sky. The solar path is the means of your rise. To look higher, to believe in higher, is your way forward.

The solar path is devotion to greatness, power, and glory. Make no mistake, greatness, power, and glory is something every man seeks. That too, is in the blood. Even the commies believe that by making everything equal, they will rise from their current place in society(because that's how low they think of themselves.)

You must ask yourself, how devoted are you? How much are you willing to sacrifice to reach your ends? The answer should be everything. Devotion to your self-creation, Devotion to your Great Work, Devotion to your legacy. These you must dwell on.

11.
HOW STRONG IS YOUR DEVOTION?

It's no understatement to say we live in a clown world. America — and the West — is a failed society. Conservatives don't conserve anything. Liberals don't fight for the working class. It's not hard to lose your way and despair in this climate. The future is uncertain. How strong is your devotion amongst this madness?

Devotion hits me hard every time I hear or read the word, especially as an American. It's a spiritual power word. Devotion is non-stop dedication to something important to you. It's a way of living with purpose. You know — what every American claims to want in a job. They claim to want to make a difference. To have some fulfilling career. It's all fake and what they think teacher wants to hear.

The real pandemic isn't this chinese AIDS floating around, it's the uncontrollable division of the former United States. The causes are many. At its core, however, I believe the true cause to be the stark decline of testosterone and the war on men. I've spent my best years having to undo the criminal indoctrination of my upbringing by institutions and misguided family members. It's my goal to get this message out to as many as I can so that they don't have to waste years trying to figure out the meaning of life or what it means to be a man.

If you look at your prospects and only see despair, I have some words for you. The American Way you're seeing isn't the true American Way. It's a fiction developed by the left in the 1960s. They say the business of America is business, but now it's social justice, BLM, and LGBT. The reality for red-blooded Americans is much different. The left wants you to believe that everyone is a potential American and we have no right to deny them access to America. They are wrong.

America was formed by civic nationalism. There's an argument to be made that ethnic nationalism creates stronger bonds between people — and I believe this, but that's just not how America was founded. Today, however, there is a civic and ethnic connection to the idea of America. You can migrate to America and be American, but for this to be true, in your heart you must feel like you were born in the wrong country(like how the trans is born in the wrong body).

This civic vision of nationalism cannot be replicated by modern leftists. To be a leftist today is to be at arms against the American founding traditions. They don't want to return to tradition, they want to destroy it. The leftist doesn't believe in 1776. There are still millions who believe in the civic nationalist vision of America.

The institutions want you to believe the idea of America comes from freeing the slaves in the Civil War and saving the world — as well as the Jews — in World War II. The modern left is founded on these two moments in history. But for Founding

Stock Americans, their founding traditions are the American Revolution and the Civil War. They have family lines tracing back to America's beginning. My ancestors have been around since before the Revolution, and I have ancestors who fought in both of those wars.

If your ancestors came to America sometime after those two wars, you won't have a racial connection to America. It's more likely you are a civic nationalist or you're on the side of destroying "evil" America. Both views are distinctly American and have a place in the conversation. There's also a deeper vision I have about Founding Stock Americans that must be known. I want all despairing Founding Stock to read these words of power.

I began this essay by asking, "How strong is your devotion?" I strongly believe for some of us that devotion is in the blood. When I took the time to learn about my bloodline, I came to a great truth. American Founding Stock comes primarily from ancestral lines originating from England and Europe. My ancestors have always been on the frontier. My last name is of old Germanic origin. My people likely migrated from Germany to France, Belgium, and then eventually to England and Scotland.

They were among the first settlers of America. They came as outlaws and outcasts. My ancestors migrated from Virginia to California. They fought in the Civil War. In fact, my last name became what it is today in the aftermath of the Civil War. Perhaps, it was changed to escape the old pre-Civil War life as one of my ancestors moved west in search of power and freedom. He was, after all, on the losing side. Why suffer in the reconstruction when you can go west into the frontier?

I feel a real connection to the frontier — in my blood. Recently, I saw some thread of people complaining about White people climbing mountains. What's up with that? Perhaps, in our blood, there's some innate desire to go out into the unknown, to turn the wheel of mankind. To seek out greatness, power, and glory as Jünger said. Maybe our strength isn't in civilization, but out on the frontier.

My people were meant to go beyond the edge of civilization. Do the hard things, lay the groundwork. Maybe it's in my blood to desire conquest, to desire power and freedom. Climbing a mountain is just the modern expression of this. They like to call the founders evil colonizers, but they were men of power. They lived in hard times with high attrition to lay the groundwork for this country. Modern leftists would die out long before accomplishing anything like they did.

Maybe the blood of the Founding Stock desires adventure and conquest. We will continue to live on the frontier until our bloodlines discover the next great empire. Or, the battle between right and left is just boring. The frontier offers what civilization cannot: the opportunity for greatness, power, and glory.

When I ask you how strong your devotion is, I ask you how strong your resolve is to cast away modern despair and mediocrity and how willing are you to seek out the frontier in a time where there are no unknown lands. Make no mistake, the frontier is out there.

PART II:

REAL AMERICANS

12.
YOUR AMERICAN MASTERS

I. American Empire and the Global Elite

Technology is allowing mankind to live a fabricated reality. But in order to keep that fabrication, men must be taught to abandon the instincts found in the blood. I talk here primarily about the American Empire and its "soft" rule over many countries through the ideal of western liberal democracy.

The sad reality, if you're strong enough to look beyond the mainstream narrative, is that America is less a democracy and more of an oligarchy. Many claim to believe this, nobody disputed it — even Americans — but we as people have yet to internalize it. Despite knowing the game is rigged by the elite, the vast majority of Americans still run around talking about how they must protect their liberal democracy or how such and such is a threat to their liberal democracy.

It takes a strong heart to address reality, but the constitution of the American people has grown weak since the USA took the position of empire over the modern world. What most Americans don't understand is the extent of their indoctrination under the American Empire. They believe in the oligarchy, but not the psychological conditioning they've been raised under. They like to point at the global elite as a bunch of trust fund kids destroying America because they're greedy. The fact of the matter is they don't know who the elite really are or what they've done.

The elite remain largely unknown and that's how they want to keep it. You think them greedy trust fund kids, but it goes far beyond this. The elite are the masters and as masters, they've learned from the mistakes of previous slave holders. Meanwhile, you and the rest of Americans, are still caught up in our "problematic" past. Get with the times!

II. Slavery never really ended.

We Americans like to talk about how we ended slavery and freed the blacks in the Civil War. On the same tongue, you'll hear Americans curse the rebels who tried to keep the institution alive without knowing that they too, are slaves. What? How can I say this? The Civil War was fought between two elite groups over the direction(wealth and power) of the country at the cost of hundreds of thousands of Americans like you and me. It wasn't fought over slavery. The decision to free the slaves was made near the end of the war.

The world is governed by men of power and the elites of the Civil War era saw the writing on the wall for slavery. The world was becoming more advanced, more sophisticated. Look at the French Revolution. Great western liberal democracy came into being there and the elites were put to the guillotine. Did you not think the rest of the world — and the men of power at the time — did not see this? What you must understand about the elite is that they're already many steps ahead of you.

The French Revolution likely taught the elite that if they were to survive the coming age, they would have to live in the shadows. They would also revolutionize slavery in ways we're still subjected to today. It can be said that the end of America — the romanticized version of it we know — ended with the Civil War.

III. Modern Slavery in America

In a world where slavery is looked down upon, the elite had to find another way to compound their wealth and power. This was done in two ways: subverting the American Republic and going underground. The American subversion was done in several steps. Freeing the slaves allowed employers to charge their employees less, a strategy which would be continued in the future with women's rights and policies like open borders.

Americans like to believe that America is a melting pot where anyone can come and pull themselves up by the bootstraps. But this is a new idea that came out of 1965 and not something the founders had in mind. How does this make you feel?

No, open borders is a terrible policy that only hurts the poor and middle class Americans while making the elite that much richer. It makes you feel good to want open borders so you can give third worlders a better life. Damn, if that doesn't make you feel morally superior, I don't know what to tell you. The problem however is that you don't just take it like the morally superior man you are, you complain about the billionaires being too greedy while you are making the necessary sacrifice to make space for asylum seekers.

All you're doing by letting everyone in is further damage your future and the future your children. The elite aren't going to see anything but upside to open borders. More people mean more customers, more wealth. They don't have to deal with the people you let in. There's really no downside for them. Diversifying America actually makes the elite stronger, not as a collective.

Jeff Bezos, the founder of Amazon and owner of Whole Foods, monitors the diversity in his stores. Why? Certainly, diversity is our strength so maybe diverse stores gave him better profit and a happier workforce? Nope. What Bezos found is the more diverse the store, the less likely it would try to unionize again him. What's that? Yes, diversity has nothing to do with "our strength." It's just a means of holding you down. Does it make sense why diversity and HR departments are sprouting up everywhere like weeds?

Before you call me racist, you must know that I grew up in a hard liberal family and was indoctrinated by the same education system you were. I've internalized Martin Luther King's idea of judging a man by his character, not his skin color. Come at me.

This is a big part of the elites subversion of America. I remember learning from somewhere that early human tribes regarded foreigners as less than human because they looked different then them. Yeah, they could still be backstabbed by a tribesman or someone that looks like them, but men aren't perfect creatures. They liked what was similar and distrusted anything that was different. This was an evolutionary adaptation that helped them survive. We, in the modern world, still make use of this adaptation — even though we know it to be wrong.

It's not just White people who are racist, everyone is to different extents. The way this works in the workplace is clear. You, being educated(indoctrinated), understand that diversity is our strength, HOWEVER, you also know that different people come from different cultures with different values. You also know it's popular to hate America right now, so us being united by nationality will not save you.

Knowing these things to be true, you're less likely to confide in your coworkers about the injustices done against you by corporate because they might actually be dirty rats who will report you to Human Resources. This lets Jeff Bezos screw you and everyone else over without any fear of retribution. You need only imagine scaling this idea to America. What are you doing by encouraging mass immigration to the United States? Ensuring that the elite will continue to screw you over and laugh as you try to rebel against their injustices.

A diverse people distrust one another, allowing for the elite ruling over them to compound their wealth and power at the expense of the poor and middle classes. When you have many different cultures squished into one country it's easy to keep the people divided. They will kill each other long before they discover how badly they've been betrayed by the elite. Divided and conquered is the state of modern Americans and western liberal democracy.

IV. You don't know who they are.

In the midst of this chaos that's America 2020, if you can bring yourself to see and believe what I see and believe, you have no outlet. You don't know who the elite are. Sure, there are some names you might know, but you have no access to them. Furthermore, anyone you might rally to your side is too busy fighting in the weeds with the rest of the slaves over micro-aggressions, perceived racism, and social justice to see the threat we all face. They'll call you a conspiracy theorist or crazy. The masters are untouchables.

This is the state of America 2020 and there is no drastic change you can do today or tomorrow that will change this. You must sow the foundations of a better society with strong hearts and a stronger constitution. This war against the oligarchs will not be won tomorrow, you must play the long game and you must play to win. They are many steps ahead of you.

The way forward will take time, it will be arduous. Society must become stronger and more united to take on the global elite. This, I believe, won't be done in our generation unless something drastic happens. Even then, it may be too soon. It's important in these times to do as BAP suggests, find friends. Loyalty is the most important trait to look for. Better still, find people who share your beliefs(they most likely will look like you based on what we now know about diversity).

Go and live in communities that share your values. This is the first step to becoming powerful. You and your friends and your community must be united against them terrible practices of the elite. To do this, you must separate from the mainstream economy and create your own eco-system within the empire. This must be kept under wraps as much as possible. Work in the shadows to make this happen. It doesn't take the entirety of America to bring down the elites, you need only a few dozen men of power.

The most important thing you can do is to become a man of power or have sons, in hopes that you can inspire them to become men of power. I would say that it is much easier to convince your sons, if you practice what you preach.

13.
WHAT IS THE REAL AMERICA?

What is America? Modern leftists claim America is this beacon of liberal democracy. Anyone can be American. Anyone should be able to become American. Anyone can immigrate to America so long as they embrace the modern American values of BLM, LGBT, Equality, and Social Justice.

America reached the world stage by building weapons for Europe during both world wars and then showing up at the critical moments to turn the tide — just like you would see in the old WWF days when Stone Cold would appear out of nowhere to deliver a stone cold stunner or break a chair over somebody's head. It then used its new influence to export Coca-Cola and Rock N Roll to the world. Modern America continues this storied tradition of export — only now it's trans lgbt gender studies.

Was America always meant to become this? Perhaps. The Founders just wanted to be equal to their British counterparts. Read about George Washington and much of his ire comes from how he didn't get paid the same as his British counterparts in the military or how lower-ranked British officers would treat him like a second-class citizen. He was oppressed you see!

But unlike modern Americans, Washington and the other founders earned their freedom. The system they put into its place wasn't so different — it just benefited them, not the Empire. I'd argue the American Revolution, the Founding Fathers, and the Constitution are not the spirit of the real America. What is the real America? The frontier and the men born from it.

Life on the frontier was the real America. Life on the frontier was tough. Colonial villages could die out. You could be scalped during an Indian raid. The colonists who lived in America had to become tough and ruthless to survive. Life on the frontier built grit in colonial Americans to withstand the greatest army in the world at the time. Washington himself experienced the frontier. He was a surveyor of land in Virginia, and he had many adventures in the frontier before taking command of the Continental Army.

Mountain men, trappers, frontiersmen, rangers, and cowboys are the real America. Their efforts helped shape the United States we know today. Their sons fought in the wars that took the USA to the world stage. Germans during WWI said much about the Americans they fought. They were impressed by

American boldness and courage. They were surprised to see how big Americans were as well as the craftsmanship of American equipment. The frontier made America strong. Were Americans smart enough to realize this, journeys into the frontier would be modern rites of passage for young men.

Forget the Founding Fathers, the Constitution, or the warped modern narrative of American history. Prove your worth on the frontier. If you want to feel what it's like to live in the real America, you must escape civilization and go into the frontier. Find a worthy challenge. Climb a mountain, venture into Death Valley, see Colorado or Montana. Do something hard. Do something that will remind you that you're still alive. Do something to prove your power and vitality.

14.
THE WHITE QUESTION

The horror of White supremacy and racism is the fad of our age. There's a significant majority of the United States population that truly believes White supremacy and racism are THE main threats to "our democracy." Granted — you only need to look at the facts to see if there is any truth to this assertion. Is White culture celebrated? Is it celebrated like the establishment celebrates BLM, LBGTQ tranny, or woke culture?

What is the more likely scenario? A White getting fired for claiming to hate black people or a black getting fired for claiming to hate White people? Anyone with just an ounce of reasoning capacity knows the answer to this.

It's not politically correct to embrace White culture as a White person. To do so is to be racist towards "people of color." Even if you don't have any prejudices towards them. Understand — this is how the world works now. If you are White, you must internalize guilt from the actions of your ancestors. Ancestors who you didn't know or understand. You must feel guilty for White colonialism — even though you played no part in it. You must sacrifice your opportunities in life for POC because of this.

And if you're black or a person of color, you must celebrate your culture. Be proud. If you don't succeed at first, it's not your fault. You're not responsible for yourself. You're a victim of evil White supremacy. As President Joe Biden said, poor kids can be just as talented as White kids.

If you buy into this logic, I tell you that you've been brainwashed. Feminists, LGBTQ, trans, and the like have been given a fake sense of entitlement. They've been empowered by the establishment so the establishment can continue to screw over the American Founding Stock. America is being milked dry by oligarchs. Both left and right know this, but they're both in on it.

If you're White, you've been brainwashed into feeling guilty for crimes you did not commit. The term White is an American term. It's derogatory in a sense as how do you classify White? German? Anglo-Saxon? European? Scottish? Irish? Russian? Scandinavian? You're liquidating all those distinct cultures when you say White. I can't speak to other peoples because I'm not them nor have I cared enough to educate myself. I can only speak to my experience and the people in my circle. And what I can tell you is Americans are being mindfucked.

I'm sick and tired of hearing about White supremacy and racism. I dream of an actual DIVERSE world where every race and culture can celebrate their race and culture without stigma and judgment. This is real diversity. What you think is diversity is not at all. It's just the looting of US citizens.

If you're White and you're reading this, I encourage you to research your ancestry. American culture has become degenerate in every sense, but you will find pride in your ancestry — especially when you learn your story. How you got to where you are. American education does little more than indoctrinate and create mental prisons you spend the best years of your life trying to escape.

What is happening to the American Founding Stock is not right or just. If you grew up in America, you've been raised under an American mythology(not history) designed to subjugate you. They want you to embrace slave morality. And they do this by making you believe slavery is over.

The American mythology is this idea — taught as historical fact in school — that America was founded by racist White colonists who weren't that great. BUT Founding Stock Americans redeemed themselves by freeing the slaves during the Civil War and defeating the evil Confederates. And then, almost a hundred years later, the United States goes on to defeat the evil fascist Nazi Empire and save the Jews.

Yes, that's right. Now we're becoming a more tolerant society by pushing to the forefront the peoples really responsible for American exceptionalism and ingenuity: LGBT biracial peoples of color. They have made America what it is despite the vast majority of Founding Stock Americans who make up the population. At the time of this writing, it was around 60% of the population. During the American mythology, the number was closer to 80-90%.

Now many leftists who read this will believe my words to be hateful. They will use them against me if they could. I don't care who you are or what you believe. You can live how you want to live — that's what America is supposedly really about. But you must also let me do the same or we're going to have problems. Everyone has seen the "I just wanted to grill" meme. I believe we are past that stage now.

This is directed at the Founding Stock who have been told since childhood to fear their own nature. You must fear your innate tOxIc MaScUliNiTy. You must check your White privilege. All of this is bullshit. You've done nothing wrong. Harboring such sentiments is detrimental to your own mental and physical health. Harboring such sentiments stunts your potential for growth, and to live a fulfilling life.

There is a reason obesity is out of control. There is a reason mental illness is out of control. All these preachers of liberal democracy and education are feeding you bullshit. Of course — they, being true believers, buying into bullshit doesn't make it any less bullshit. As Nietzsche said, "the preachers of equality are tarantulas."

Everything that will make you strong and powerful, courageous and honorable is discouraged if not outright banned. It's sexist to have a men's groups. Confidence and manliness are "problematic." Men should be more like women. White people should step aside for POC. This is all garbage. It's all psychological warfare to crush Founding Stock Americans and give more power to the oligarchs raping the country.

LGBTQ trans or woke people are being USED by the establishment to the detriment of us all. My message isn't for them, however. My message is for the Founding Stock that's being mindfucked. You must reject the establishment. You must reject modern Americanism. This consumerist culture left us all fat and degenerate.

Founding Stock Americans must undo the damage. Turn off the news. Hell, turn off social media. Connect offline and support each other. Powerlift. Become strong as fuck. Create your own businesses instead of being a thrall to some corporation that's probably fucking America over behind the scenes.

Men must return to nature, return to their nature. Manliness is not toxic. Lack of manliness is. Nothing gets you back to nature faster than physical culture. Lift heavy weights, take up boxing, and go on hikes. Do this with your friends. Form friendships. Start your own groups, gangs, brotherhoods, and war bands. Take oaths of brotherhood forge cults of strength. Connect with like-minded men. Embrace your bloodlines. This has less to do with supremacy(but you should be striving for superiority) and more about honoring your ancestors. Imagine the times they had to survive just to make that possible.

On that same note, have sons. Many sons. Don't abort your bloodline because of what's happening in the world. That's the coward's way out. Become strong and teach your children to become strong. Trust what's in your blood, your ancient instincts won't lead you astray. Modern mental illness derives from the smothering of your ancient instincts by oppressive liberal institutions. If you can't sense what's in the blood, start with physical culture and it will reveal itself to you.

It's not enough to do everything I said above, there is one more requirement to get out of this hell. The reason why America is like this is because the Founding Stock chose tolerance over power. The side of LGBTQ-trans-woke chose power over tolerance. You and your friends must be absolutely intolerant of anything and anyone that threatens your culture. You must choose strength over going along to get along. Being passive is weakness. And weakness IS evil.

What's good is strength and power and courage. Make no mistake, we're in enemy territory now. Act accordingly. While you chase power, you must operate underground like a guerrilla. Stay under the radar while you build strength.

15.
BLOODLINES AND WHAT IS AMERICAN?

Early on in my life, I didn't give a shit about my ancestry. Never asked my parents about it or anything. Didn't care — I was an American, that's it. For the most part, I blame this on my typical American commie indoctrination. You learn so much about how evil the Confederates and Nazis were in history class, you don't want to look back into your own ancestry because what if you're related to em? I wanted to believe my bloodline was storming the beaches of Normandy, not defending them. Like everyone, I wanted to be heroic and of heroic lineages. Becoming a father changes your perspective.

Going through life not knowing or caring about heritage is a detriment. Not knowing your heritage is how the leviathan mindfucks you into carrying out it's will. With no history, the leviathan makes one for you, one that supports whatever ends they have.

A couple years ago, knowing I had a son on the way, it suddenly mattered to me. What if he asks me where we came from? It seemed childish to hold the same views I had before. What had kept me from researching my bloodline and heritage before was fear of shame. What if my ancestors were bad men? Yes, the leviathan manufactures White guilt and White hatred in Americans. They use race as a means of control. Keep us at each other's throats.

So, I deep dived in the cheapest way I can. I started with google searches to dig into my paternal bloodline. Luckily for me, my last name isn't common and so I found out much just by using google. If you have a common last name, it will not be so easy. My dad was from a small town in Northern California. So small, he attended the same school from kindergarten to high school. My family had been there for 3-4 generations after moving west from Texas. Before my Texas, my family was in Mississippi, South Carolina, and Virginia.

One of my forefathers fought for the Confederates. This was what I was afraid of as a punk kid, but now it's a point of pride. Another ancestor fought in the Revolutionary War. My paternal and maternal lines have been in America since before the Revolution.

The leviathan through academia teaches that America is an idea. Anyone can be American. You just have to have American values which today means you want to bomb some third world country to bring democracy and tranny rights to their schools. The two most important American moments for the leviathan agenda are the Civil War and the holocaust. These events are used to unite "Americans" against the Founding Stock who still hold some power in the country.

The actual pinnacle events for the Founding Stock are the Revolutionary War and the Civil War (but for different reasons). The leviathan seeks to portray the Founding Stock as evil White colonizers who have committed great sins against humanity. Any ancestors of Whites should live forever ashamed of their history. They should forego their own prosperity so some minority can prosper in their place.

America hasn't been around long compared to other empires, but it's been around long enough for there to be genetic diversity between the Europeans who migrated here and who we are today. Founding Stock Americans are in a sense — a new race.

It's worth noting that after a brutal Civil War, the Confederates were brought back into the Union. Many historians praise the battle prowess and leadership of the Confederates. Read about Stonewall Jackson, Nathan Bedford Forrest, and John S. Mosby. Military bases were named after

Confederates. Statues were built. These were all made by Americans who participated and suffered because of the Civil War. But now we live in an age where Americans with no ancestral connection or understanding of that event want to tear it all down.

The night I spent researching my paternal line sticks with me to this day. It made me realize that your bloodline — whoever you are — is important. Your lineage stretches all the way back to the first men, to the beginning of mankind. You owe it to your ancestors to continue the line. How many disasters, plagues, wars, or hardships did your bloodline have to endure to make you? It was a surreal experience to see how my bloodline moved across the United States and to piece together where they were before. If I could I'd want to trace it all back to the beginning.

The ancient Pagans saw the worst crimes imaginable as either betraying The Gods or betraying your people or nation. These crimes were worst then murder or rape. What you're seeing right now is a part of the Founding Stock betraying their own people. While the dark schemes are the work of the leviathan, we who do nothing to right the wrong also shoulder the blame.

America is a young country, but your bloodline is old. All our current America problems aside, our bloodlines are old. It's important to figure out where you come from, what your ancestors believed in, and what your last name means.

In many essays on RESAVAGER, I've talked about "what's in the blood" as BAP says. The way you are is related to the experiences of your ancestors. It's possible how we think and what we believe is directly related to the experience of our bloodlines. Digging into your ancestral history may reveal to you why you do things one way or the other. One example of this. When I took martial arts, my style was often compared to a bear. That I turned into a bear when I sparred. Come to find out, the proto-meaning of my name has something to do with a bear. I have strong desire to go out into nature, into the unknown. Explore new places. Is it coincidence that I was born in California? California marked the end of the American frontier and for the most part, the end of the unknown world.

Many Americans are being separated from their heritage. It's gotten so bad that many are choosing not to have kids and are voluntarily ending their bloodlines. This is shameful and a great betrayal to their people. If you are anything like me and grew up without a care about your ancestry, I urge you to reconsider. Talk to your parents and grandparents if you can. Unfortunately, I didn't get the chance to talk to mine. Take a DNA test and see where your blood comes from. Who are your people? What did they believe in? You must discover this.

16.
OUR PRINCIPLES, THEIR HYPOCRISY!

This is an ode to the "blood-red conservative." The American obese who believes in freedom, equality, and the 2nd Amendment. You know of who I speak, the ones who spout much of what we believe but don't look the part. They believe themselves on the moral high ground. They believe in a merit-based culture. They don't see skin color. What matters is in the constitution. USA is the greatest country in the world, amirite? The real problem is the lazy hippie leftists who don't want to work and think all money should be siphoned from the 1%. It's their damn socialist policies that are destroying the country and the middle class.

The Republican Party and all their followers think somehow, they're going to save the country by sticking to their morals and principles. Most importantly, they call out the left's hypocrisy because that's what going to stick it to them. Even though they disagree entirely with what the left is saying, damn it, they will defend their right to say it. This is the way, right?

Conservatives are controlled opposition. Republicans think they're having spirited debates with fellow Americans(they're not). Republicans think they're arguing with equals(they're not). Republicans somehow believe, after the mountain of evidence saying otherwise, that the left has the same standard that they do(they don't). Republican politicians disappoint their party again and again, but Republicans still vote for them.

The left isn't playing by the same rules. They don't think they're having spirited debates. They believe they're fighting for their lives. They don't think they're equals, they believe Republicans are bigoted and racist, morally evil demons to be killed. They're playing for power. They're playing to win.

The country continues to drift toward a leftist hellscape because the Republican Party is simply controlled opposition and the people who vote for them, keep voting for them. Conservatives give the left the frame and the power. Any debates or seats at the table are only granted if conservatives agree to the leftist frame, to accept their point of view at the expense of their own. Conservatives are reduced to attacking their constituents to show they're morally just and have principles.

Meanwhile, their constituents who make up a good half of the population get shit on. Not just by the left, but by gop as well. Their interests are made to be morally evil. Their religion attacked as backward and bigoted. They're made out to be uneducated and stupid.

The right forgot its agency. It's been so long since the right has thought about its own interests that most people who identify as right-leaning are only on damage control. They just don't want to be called racists or Nazis. Who cares if your way of life is going down the toilet?

Every race is entitled to celebrate and be proud of their culture, except for White people. The Founding Stock must be ashamed of their ancestors and history. Any celebration of their accomplishments is White supremacy. What the hell is this ride and how do I get off? The right is playing a generations-long game of appeasement with the left, thinking it's all about to go back to normal so long as they accept whatever the next concession is. If you're on the right, stop the insanity.

What the hell is the right even fighting for? The only thing you see Republican politicians fighting for is not to be called names like racist or Nazi or fascist. And they're losing. So, let me explain to you what you should be fighting for. And fighting like your life depends on it. You're fighting for survival. You're fighting for your life and mine. Your family and your friends' lives. American culture has been systematically destroyed. It would be unrecognizable to any American just a generation ago.

It's happened right under our noses and the very institutions you trust the most are responsible. The schools have turned your children against you. Poisoned their minds with unnatural leftoid ideologies. Corporations poison your food and water in the name of growing their profit margins. Your government profits off you while watering down any power you had to a massive influx of immigrants.

The people that do this don't care about leftists. They don't believe the bullshit they spout. What they care about is these leftists hating you with every fiber of their body so they will go out of the way to take all the power from Founding Stock Americans. The people who rule over you only care about money and power. They don't care about your home, your family, or your country.

The things the left wants you to be ashamed of are nothing but commie propaganda. Yes, to be ashamed about the things that leftists want you to be ashamed about doesn't make you a morally superior human being. The right has only accepted their frame of thought. If anything, you've accepted propaganda that'll make your culture easier to conquer.

Don't believe me? If you're familiar with Los Angeles, you can get an idea of what I'm talking about. Armenians stick together. There's Chinatown and Korea-town, etc. Same with blaqs and Mexicans. They have their own cultures and don't deny what's in the blood. It's not that they hate one race or the other, they just trust their own first. Is this right? No, but it's human nature.

Whites have been targeted by the regime to be "de-powered." You can say whatever you want to a White and face almost no consequences. This ain't racism though. Whites are moral demons who have oppressed mankind since the beginning of time. Is any of this starting to sound familiar? You have Yale professors openly talking about dreams where they get to murder Whites. If you don't fight for your life now what the odds of the next "holocaust" will be against Whites?

You have a right to be proud of your people, your ancestors, and your culture — but ONLY if you're willing to defend them with MIGHT. Whites don't become evil by honoring the culture they came out of. It doesn't make them "supremacists." Are Whites evil superior to anything anymore? We look pretty damn pacified to me. This is not how you preserve your people and your culture. This is not how you preserve the country you claim to love. Pride is a word stolen from you and given to the undeserving. But if you don't reclaim it, you don't deserve it either.

Evil is a perspective. It comes from a subjective point of view. It's not an eternal concept. What the left claims is evil is by design meant to disempower Whites. What Whites held slaves? Hell, every race under the sun has been slaves as well as masters. Religion is a piece of human nature. Leftists believe they escaped religion with science, but they've simply made science their religion. They're just as dogmatic and intolerant as what they imagine the Christian to be.

This is your way of life and you're letting the leftists and their overlords take it from you. Will you continue down the dead-end road of Our Principles, Their Hypocrisy?! Or will you stand and fight?

17.
REAL AMERICAN

The past two years have been a shit show in America. There appear to be two sides with irreconcilable differences forming. While this hasn't changed any, the last two Fourth of July celebrations have been sparks of hope. Despite all the psychological campaigns being waged against red-blooded Americans, that American spirit still comes out on July 4th. Any anti-Americanism on the 4th take is found in bad taste and easily identifies our enemies.

You can distinguish the Real American from the pretenders and traitors on the 4th. There's not a whole lot to be proud of in America today, but the Real American Spirit still flickers in our proudest moment: George Washington delivering a Stone Cold Stunner to a red coat during the War for Independence and talking about his neck routine to his fellow patriots.

Meanwhile, our real enemies reveal themselves. Exhibit A is our current President talking about the way of showing your real patriotism is taking the vaccine. Hell no, that ain't what being a Real American is about. A Real American gives the finger to the empire and unleashes America in all her Glory. He's letting the red, white, and blue run wild in the name of Freedom. Real Americans are rebels, outlaws, cowboys, and frontiersmen who have a problem with authority. The colonists put everything on the line to break free from outside influence. To live how they wanted to live.

The future looks bleak for Real Americans. The independence our forefathers fought for is threatened. I remember the 4th of 2020 well. In the height of rona hysteria, nightly news helicopters flew over the city to find so many illegal fireworks being set off, it looked like a war zone. Even in the leftist shithole of LA, the Real American spirit is strong.

Real Americans let their fire and passion show on the 4th. It's something however, that can't be saved for just the 4th if you want to save this country. This attitude must ring from coast to coast and any who would try to snuff it out must be soundly crushed. The American Way is the way of the frontier. The colonists existed on the edge of what was the known world. They found a way to survive and thrive. You owe it to your ancestors to honor the legacy they left for you.

The way forward may mean leaving the American Empire as we know it today. It may mean returning to the frontier. It may mean a valiant last stand that will be remembered in the ages to come. No one can say. No matter what happens you must remember the fire of the Real American Spirit.

Are you a Real American?

18.
MOSBY'S RANGERS SHALL RIDE AGAIN

Colonel John S. Mosby and his Rangers plagued the Union supply and communication lines during the Civil War to such effect, many thought Mosby didn't even exist at all — he was a myth. A tall story. A boogeyman. Union soldiers could find no evidence of him even being real. The three Virginian counties he operated in were known as Mosby's Confederacy. Union commanders believed he had thousands of Calvary at his back, but his partisan operations were often done with only a couple hundred.

After Robert E. Lee surrendered the Army of Northern Virginia, Confederate soldiers were all offered parole — all of them except Colonel John S. Mosby. That's how much hatred and fear he seared into the minds of those he terrorized in the North. There was much fear that Mosby wouldn't surrender, that he and his Rangers would become guerrillas. But some six months after Lee, Mosby surrendered, one of the last Confederates to do so.

The Memoirs of Colonel John S. Mosby is a must-read.

Modern society goes out of its way to demonize anything that threatens the holy grail of racism. The mob rages against history they know nothing about. The North for example believed Mosby shouldn't have been paroled. He should have been hanged. But Mosby himself also believed slavery should be outlawed. He fought for the Confederacy because he was fighting to protect his family, friends, and state, not to uphold slavery. Mosby fought for his mother state, Virginia.

After the Civil War, he became a good friend of Ulysses S. Grant and even sparked the outrage of the South by voting for Grant to become president. The South had adored Mosby up to that point and this was seen as a deep betrayal. There's much to learn from Colonel Mosby that the left will throw aside because he fought on the wrong side. The value of reading Mosby is too high to be ignored. Much of the media put out today is made to virtue signal transBIPOCalphabet groups at the expense of actual men. This type of media is boring and far from believable.

I've gotten more lessons from men of power and adventure. How powerful and exciting is it to read about Ernst Jünger rescuing his brother in the middle of a battle in The Great War? Or is Peter Kemp doing everything he can to get into World War II just to find himself recruited into the first Special Forces operations? You want to hear about men like you doing great things. For Americans who have been too long separated from their history, there's no better time than now to reconnect with our proud heritage. Many of these "Americans" who trash the founders or the Confederacy to virtue signal didn't show up in the country until after World War II.

Mosby went beyond his rank, he didn't just do his job, but he looked for openings to forward the Southern Cause. This he called being a partisan. Partisan held a different meaning during the Civil War. To be a partisan was to be a guerrilla. Many at the time didn't respect partisan warfare. To be called a guerrilla was to be insulted. But Mosby didn't take offense to the term. He believed everything he did was as a soldier and within the rules of war at the time. He forced Union armies to commit so many troops to their rear to protect against his Rangers, he kept the Confederacy in the war longer.

I propose that the men on our side today take up a similar kind of PARTISAN WARFARE. There's much Civil War and national divorce talk today, though we're in less of a position to win than the Confederates were. If this is a battle you truly want to win, you must engage in partisan operations against the enemy. You must become — as Mosby did — a nightmare in their minds. A tall tale, a scary story. But you must also be the force hitting the leviathan where it's weakest. Starving it of supplies and communication.

Your actions should devastate the leviathan without ever presenting a target. This is war, but not by the means most on the right want to engage in. They want pitched battles with opportunities for honor and glory. What is actually needed though is culture, friendships, and brotherhoods. Real relationships with the people in your communities as well as the complete and utter discrediting of the regime and its propaganda.

Mosby's Rangers shall ride again. Mosby and his men damn near supplied the entire Confederacy. They took food, clothing, arms, and horses to send back to the armies. The Union blockade prevented supply and trade in the South. The South was nowhere near as industrialized as the North. Men like Mosby or Nathan Bedford Forrest not only did their jobs, they took care of their men like family. Many flocked to fight under them because they knew they would get their chance for honor, glory, and adventure. These men left their commands better off than when they found them. Mosby had his Rangers in the very best Union gear and arms. You must adopt this kind of mindset if you hope to leave any mark on the world.

What makes you think you'll win another Civil War if you can't get men to follow you? If you can't find the path to succeed under the current conditions, you aren't going to do anything of worth. Excel in the life The Gods have provided for you and make the lives of those around you better because of you. This is where powerful resistance rises from.

Mosby was known as the Gray Ghost during the war. He'd ravage the supply lines, intercept valuable communications, and rout superior forces. All while the Union wasn't sure the man existed at all. At one point, there was a $5,000 bounty put on his head. This doesn't seem like a big number now but think in terms of the value of the dollar during the Civil War era(over a hundred thousand dollar bounty).

Master the space around you and leave everything better than you found it. Be like Mosby.

19.
PALEFACE PREPAREDNESS

We live in time of crisis. It doesn't always feel like it, but its presence is there, sometimes hidden in the shadows. Subconsciously, most realize society is being set up for collapse. There are no better eyes that can see this than through the eyes of a boy as our education system(indoctrination camp) rips his soul from him. Even common sense ain't common anymore. Try to fight out of the path we're on and the full power of the state will be brought down upon your skull.

The desire to be heroic is present in all men. This desire makes a "good man" want to stand up to injustice. Be an ally for the weak and downtrodden. Be some light in the darkness. This is how the normal man is conditioned during his formative years. He's taught how to be heroic in an age of heroes, but we don't live in the age of heroes. The age we live in is an age of snakes. These men are being set up to either be crushed by the state or turned into a coward.

The type of men being raised aren't capable of victory. They're designed to be good cattle for their masters and if any of them are brave enough to rebel, the state crushes them like a cockroach. What keeps any meaningful resistance is our disconnection from nature. Most men are brought up on false pretenses about the world and nature. Our masters don't have such pretenses and where they might, it's masked by their power.

Before you can resist the system, you have to understand how the world works and what it means to be a man. Might is right is natural law. The victor determines what's right and what's wrong. If you think the world is fucked up and you don't have the power to change it — woe to the conquered. For Americans, this is especially hard to understand because you're raised to believe you're free. But you're far from free, you're a slave to the system. It's naive to believe the American system isn't co-opted by now.

There is a natural hierarchy in the world. This too, will frustrate Americans who believe everyone is equal. This pecking order can be changed, but you have to first know your place in it. Right now if you're a PALEFACE(as James LaFond calls White men), you're near the bottom of the food chain. No matter how right or heroic you imagine your resistance, the system will make it look like a despicable taboo. The world isn't governed by logic and reason. Your enemies will ignore both if it means they get to crush you.

You're behind enemy lines and you're being hunted. You have to fight as such. Sure — you can make your last stand if you're happy with that memory being co-opted by the media who will turn you into some kind of coward terrorist. Your best course of action at this time is to devote yourself to strength and power, the type of strength and power relevant to nature. To make friends you can count on in the worst situations and to free as many as you can from the mental slavery the system puts you through in your formative years. The state needs only the smallest reason to go after you. Look back to Ruby Ridge or even more recently to the FBI going after parents for speaking out against covid measures being enforced against their children as proof of this.

I understand the desire to fight and the will to fight is very important to have, but victory must be on your mind. Recently, I listened to Myth of the 20th Century podcast with James LaFond entitled "Waking Up in Indian Country." In last half, he gives powerful recommendations for preparedness for these times. I will put below my notes from the podcast. You must follow these and make yourself prepared:

1.) Do not talk to the enemy. Especially if you're being accused of racism or anything like that. Do not talk to the enemy. Do not apologize. Apologizing is affirming any kind of guilt being directed at you.

2.) Don't talk to your woman about your business. She won't be able to handle it. At best, you'll get a meltdown, and at worst.... LaFond used example of Italian mobsters. Their women surely know they're up to no good, but because they don't know the specifics, they're certain deniability the female can talk herself into. The system is designed to co-opt the woman. She will betray you if you give her the chance. Some things should remain between men.

3.) Don't let your woman pull you into a fight. If you're a paleface, there's almost no way to get out of the situation without somebody coming for your livelihood. Any woman who does this doesn't have your best interests in mind. The state is looking for palefaces to crucify.

4.) Don't talk about politics at work. This should speak for itself. There are already many examples of palefaces losing their jobs because of what they said at work or even online.

5.) Most of your family and friends will stab you in the back or turn you in, don't talk to them about this stuff. Indoctrination camps train them from very young to betray their family in service to the state. Most people in America are especially liberal, even your blood.

6.) Learn how to fight. LaFond says when you learn how to fight, you also learn the ability not to fight. I recommend serious martial arts like Boxing, BJJ, Muay Thai, or wrestling.

Learn to shoot guns. Join the military and learn modern warfare.

7.) Any paleface who uses a gun in self-defense becomes a White supremacist. Only use a gun if you plan on dying. Just look at the Rittenhouse trial. Rittenhouse didn't even kill(rightly) any poc either.

8.) Turn off the news. LaFond says it's gaslighting. The news is designed to trigger and demoralize. It's better for your morale to never watch the news.

9.) Scout your neighborhood. Know the layout of your area by walking or biking around. How can you get out if you need to? Where can you fall back to and defend? Where are the bad places to avoid? The walking also is good cardio most men don't get anymore.

If you're interested in more, listen to Myth of the 20th Century podcast for more information on being more prepared for this age of snakes. I recommend this podcast. Palefaces are disprivileged in this country, act accordingly.

PART III:

SAVING YOUR FRENS

20.
HOW TO SAVE YOUR FRIENDS FROM THE LEFTIST VIRUS

The Nietzschean Right aka The Aesthetic Right aka RW Bodybuilders aka The Surf Right holds within their movement the path to greatness, power, and glory. I will be honest with you; I grew up in democrat Christian household and it has taken time to learn from the left's wretched ways.

The problem with the left is that it eats itself and continues to move further to the left. The democrats of my youth would be considered Nazis and White supremacists to the modern left. The way of the left is the way of meekness, self-loathing, and pursuing the impossible goal of outcome equality. They are the current incarnation of the virus known as communism. The people of the left may be irredeemable.

Your primary focus should be saving as many as you can from the leftist virus, but you must take great care in how you do this. It's important to teach men the way of high vision and the rites of power, but do not frame it as a rightist view. When people think of the right, they think of the religious — Christian — right which isn't to take a dig against the Christian Right. Their religion has been co-opted by the left in many respects while also appearing as the bitter enemy to modern culture.

No, the way to lead men to salvation is to inspire their will to power.

It always begins with self-overcoming in the weight room. Lead men to the gyms. They must learn self-overcoming by getting bigger and stronger — destroying their previous personal bests again and again. By this methods, young men will learn to build. Build not just their body, but businesses and legacies. The positivity that comes from self-improvement can destroy the negativity of leftism. It is true.

When a man makes himself strong and begins to become a man of power, he is less likely to be manipulated by propaganda and values he knows as weak. Bodybuilders learn to understand their place in the food chain. To save young men, teach them self improvement and aesthetics. By simply becoming more beautiful than you are makes you incompatible with a movement that worships ugliness.

It's through this method that you show young men the way of BAP's vitality and Nietzsche's Say Yes to Life. The left lives in misery. They are always feeling oppressed, always feeling screwed over. And they hold this bitterness against the beautiful and privileged, believing they too should be able to be great--but without putting in the effort. This isn't the mentality to have if you want to live a good, glorious life.

Life is meant to be experienced. Take your friends to the beach, to the mountains, on hikes. Explore new lands. Lift together, fight together. Life is not watching Netflix or playing video game — this is place for the wretched to escape their own misery. Get out under the sun and become bronze instead.

The answer is always power. Power is what will help you achieve your goals. Power is what will destroy any leftist viral transmission to your body. This is better way to live by far.

21.
THE REAL N WORD

It only takes one generation to change society. Lenin said all he needed was one generation of youth to import Marxism into a country. The Soviet KGB dealt primarily in subversion — not espionage. Red-blooded Americans understand none of this today. If they did, they wouldn't have handed America over on a silver platter to the elites. Now I know what you're thinking, "how did this happen?" You see a good half the population rise up with bitter anti-American sentiment and maybe you got an idea. It's those damn libtards, right?!

The more I try to research and diagnose the problem — to find a solution — the deeper down the rabbit hole I go. The first step is understanding your enemy. Right and left easily just spend all their time attacking each other to no avail because they're talking past each other. The right burns its energy wailing about leftist hypocrisy meanwhile the left treats them like insane, uneducated bigots. There's no conversation, just a further divide between the two.

There may be no reconciliation between Americans. It may be too far gone, but for the red-blooded Americans still out there, I hope to help you better understand where the enemy is coming from and how you're being subverted. The Founding Leftist mythology is intermingled with the modern American Founding myths. Many of your learned beliefs about being American are intertwined with the subversion of the country.

Warped Historical Views

Modern American mythology deals less with the actual founding of America, but with two events in recent history: freeing the slaves in the Civil War and defeating the Nazis in the Second World War. This is to cement the idea that America is the pinnacle of strength and freedom. We're the good guys. Even the left — which seems to trash on strength and beauty — needs to believe that America at least has the potential to be the greatest country in the world.

The reason freeing the slaves and defeating the Nazis are so important because it makes up the bedrock of current leftist ideology. Leftist ideology is firmly rooted in Marxism and to be frank, there's no right-wing ideology in America right now. Conservatives are just liberal-light. This may be a big reason why they're failing hard. Propping up these two events as the most important in American mythology helps leftists fight conservative ideology.

The left believes that Conservatives would have been Confederates or Nazis if they were living in those times. This belief gives them powerful resolve to stand up for the perceived "weak peoples and minorities." They truly believe they're like the US soldiers who staged the Normandy landings on D-Day. The reality is they would be appalled if they learned about those soldiers' actual beliefs.

The left — and all Americans — have a warped understanding of American history. If you ask Americans why the Civil War was fought, they will tell you it was to free the slaves. The Union didn't resolve to free the slaves until the very end of the war. The Civil War was actually fought over state's rights. Lincoln is even quoted saying if he could have ended the war without freeing the slaves, he would have.

This leads us to an even bigger historical warping: World War II. Ask Americans why we fought in the Second World War and they'll tell you it was to save the Jews and people of color from the Nazis who wanted to genocide anyone who wasn't Aryan. It's widely believed the Nazis started the Second World War to exterminate the Jews. Many Americans believe the Nazis were so unhinged they would fight the world just to exterminate the Jews. Really?

The Real N Word

No, I'm not talking about THAT N word — I'm talking about Nuremberg. More specifically, the Nuremberg Trials at the end of World War II. These were tribunals meant to prosecute Nazis for their "war crimes." "Yes of course," most Americans would say. They deserved to be punished for their evil genocidal racism. The concept of war crimes, however, was unheard of before World War II.

According to OG frog, Thomas777, most people believed before the Second World War that wars came and went like the seasons. The idea that the Nazis would be punished for war crimes was seen as crazy even by United States Supreme Court justices. Many saw the Nuremberg Trials as "victor's justice" on part of the allies. After all, the Holocaust wasn't the only "war crime." War crimes had been committed by all sides.

The United States dropped two atomic bombs and firebombed most of Japan. The British firebombed much of West Germany. The US government put many Americans Japanese and Germans into internment camps. What about the millions killed by the Soviets in the interwar years(that took place on Germany's frontier, by the way)? Only the Nazis were being held to account for horrific acts done on all sides of the conflict.

What happened at Nuremberg shaped the leftist regime we see today. Not just leftists, but most Americans see the Nazis as evil incarnate. What most Americans don't know, however, is the Nuremberg Trials failed to provide evidence that the Nazis were trying to exterminate Jews because they were Jews. What made the Nazis target the Jews was their ideological leanings and the events of the interwar years which can best be described as the European Civil War.

The Russian Revolution of 1917 sparked the European Civil War. The Bolsheviks assumed power and set out to eliminate anyone who was ideologically opposed to their Marxist vision. Much of this wholesale slaughter happened in western Russia and the former German frontier. To say the Germans didn't see this happening is naive. Germany was ground zero for the Bolshevik Revolution.

The former German empire was broken up in the aftermath of the Great War. Germans were stuck in new territories that were no longer Germany. The Bolsheviks spread like a virus into these weakened states. What happened in the Second World War was less a Holocaust and more a response to the tactics of Bolshevik Russia. It was the fascists vs the communists. The Jews were seen as Bolsheviks to the core and undesirable in Nazi Germany.

We see the actions taken as horrible and inhumane by the Nazis, but we don't acknowledge that Russia was doing the same thing in the interwar years. The Nazis took notes from the Bolsheviks. This is how today the way the left tried to condemn the right is by calling them Nazis and fascists and racists. It all originated from the sham Nuremberg Trials. For a generation raised on Nazis being the ultimate evil, this is hard to see, I admit. It doesn't help when any questioning of Holocaust makes you a denier.

Fake News

Anyone who questions the Holocaust or events of World War II is immediately deemed a denier or a revisionist. They're crazy conspiracy theorists and Jew haters on the most

68

malevolent level. But how crazy is the idea really? How much of the news today is what we call fake news? Today — if a journalist doesn't name a source, the source often doesn't exist. Many false stories go viral only to find out later it didn't happen the way it was reported.

If they can get away with faking modern news, it's not hard to see how the Second World War and the Nuremberg Trials could have been mythologized. Remember, I'm not here telling you the Holocaust didn't happen — it did. I'm questioning the reasons why and explaining (not an excuse) of why it happened.

It's important to realize that the Holocaust and freeing the slaves aren't the founding mythology of America, it's just the new religion. Contrary to what leftists tell you, not everyone is a potential American. The two events that define America aren't freeing the slaves and the Holocaust, it's the Revolutionary War and the war between the states.

Americans are a race now. If your line goes back to the founding of the United States, your genetic material has changed from your European counterparts, and you see in the politics. The reason the mainstream hordes attack white America is the power they have. They make up the majority of the population and still hold much of the power. The true history of being an American is the rebellious spirit of the colonists. The frontier mindset that carried them from sea to sea. And finally, the vicious civil war which was fought primarily by white Americans on both sides.

The first Americans were exiles, rebels, and outlaws. They built the country from the ground up. They overcame nature, the Natives, and the frontier. This was no easy feat. Their efforts changed their very blood and the blood of their children. What's happened in the aftermath of the Second World War and the new religion that sprung from it has warped the American character. If this isn't corrected, America will cease to be.

It's not a long shot to see the Balkanization of the United States in the near future.

22.
THE SCHISM BETWEEN GOOD AND BEAUTIFUL

Today there is a schism between good and beautiful, one might even claim they're ideologically opposed, but this wasn't always so. The ancients associated being beautiful with being good. If you listen to BAP's Caribbean Rhythms podcast you know that the schism between good and beautiful began with Socrates. Say what you will about Socrates, but he was a *dog*. He was ugly and his name meant "smelly man," perhaps that's why he came up with what we call the Socratic Method. It was some way to justify to the Greeks that he was good despite the smell.

The modern world treats beauty and goodness as separate things. Yes, you can be beautiful-but-evil and ugly-but-good, but the idea that the two are utterly separate is folly. Goodness and beauty more often than not go hand in hand. Modern culture is full of people who are obese and weak. America — "the greatest country in the world" — has a population where 70% are considered overweight or obese. Recent events have given a glimpse at the American character. We've been revealed to be a bunch of cowards, hardly the traits of "good" people. You got a bunch of "men" who talk about how "real men don't care how they look," and a bunch of females talking about how men should love them at any size. Gross.

The progressive tolerance cult tells us we should accept all genders and body sizes so long as they're not White supremacist Nazis. The progressive way used to be to accept everyone — even if you disagree with them. But that quickly devolved into a cancel culture where 62% of US citizens are afraid to express their worldview.

Look at the pictures put forth of modern Americans. Is it something of beauty? No, it's something out of a horror flick. Fat purple-haired lesbians, men dressed as women who identify as some gender you ain't ever heard of. I don't know what cis is and I don't care. So they ain't beautiful, but are they good? You say something to offend this crowd and they will come for you. They'll figure out where you work, who you associate with, and try to dox your family. They'll try to get you fired and humiliated by mainstream media. This seems like quality good people, right? Most modern Americans are neither good nor beautiful.

Modern America is an example of how to be good, you must also be beautiful. Now — I'm not saying you have to look like Brad Pitt in <u>Troy</u> beautiful, but god damn it, take pride in your physique and style. The 300 Spartans on the night before they were to be surrounded and slaughtered at Thermopylae were seen to be bathing and brushing their hair. Look at art, statues, Ancient soldiers, warriors, and heroes and tell me they didn't care how they looked. Even the Vikings, who everyone thought were a bunch of mangy savages, took great care in grooming and working out. They were the original right-wing bodybuilders.

Your appearance matters. If you're overweight, you must lose the fat. Also, if you are skin and bones, it is time to put on muscle. It's hard to respect and take advice from someone who doesn't care about their physicality and appearance. Embarking on this quest for aesthetics will teach you what it takes to build. This lesson can be applied to every aspect of your life. Through aestheticism, through beauty, you learn how the world works. A man with an understanding of the natural order has the potential for heroism. And through heroism, you can show the quality of goodness. This is how they're related. It is possible to have one without the other, but it's rare.

More often, an ugly man doesn't have the capacity for goodness and heroism. He's chosen the path of laziness and meekness. He may think himself good, but without the testing — putting in the work — he'll be ineffective at best in a situation that requires courage. Don't internalize ugliness. The ugly and bad want to loathe the beautiful and good because they have what they don't. They want to convince themselves that because they are beautiful, there's no possible way they can be good. That would be unfair! The people who internalize ugliness are the worst.

Ugly people believe they're good because they aren't beautiful, so they have to develop other talents. This is a fallacy. You're more likely to build character by embracing physical culture — lift weights, learn to fight, and get sunlight. This will do more to make you "good" while also becoming beautiful. The ugly are just lazy.

PART IV:

TRAINING

23.
STRENGTH IS SIMPLE, BUT NOT EASY

The internet has done to lifting what science has done to culture — paralysis via information overload. One decade eggs are bad, the next decade eggs are good based on brand new study. Science has made society forget common knowledge and tradition. You might not think that important, but you should reconsider. Ideas and works that have passed the test of time don't need to be subjected to scientific inquiry. The *Iliad* is still being read, and so is The Bible — for good reason. Our ancestors knew what we had forgotten or attributed to their barbaric nature.

There are so many training programs out there. Instagram trainers are a dime a dozen. You can find all sorts of routines from simple to complex. For someone not accustomed to lifting, it can be downright confusing. Scientific inquiry calls out your name as you spend hours looking at a screen in search of the best, most advanced program to pack on muscle and lose fat. Back in the pre-internet days, training was so much simpler. Men would buy a magazine and follow the routine in there for months. If they wanted a big bench, they would bench press every day. These men wanted to be big and strong, and they willed it into existence. They were devoted to the iron. You on the other hand are just looking for the most efficient way to muscle paradise.

Quit looking for the best program and just train. There's no 30-day cure to your life of comfort. You have to put in the work, over years, trying out different strategies. The bodies you see and want to emulate didn't get that way by the Muscle & Fitness workout they published. No, these men trained for years. They were men of devotion — devotion to strength. You must find the same devotion.

Train the basic barbell lifts: the squat, bench, deadlift, and shoulder press. Pick a weight and a rep range. Train at that weight until it's easy and add more weight to the bar. My favorite is 6-10x5. If I can bust out 10 sets of 5 in half an hour, I need more weight on the bar.

Include bodyweight movements like pull-ups, dips, and lunges. It can be argued that bodyweight exercises should be the foundation of your routine. I would not argue with this. Weighted dips and lunges did more for my chest and legs than benching and squatting. And for god sake, do the mirror lifts so you look like you lift. Do your curls in for the girls. Don't tri and get bi or you will be delt with and trapped. Most importantly, train your neck so you don't get knocked out like a bitch. Get a neck harness. Do plate front and side neck raises until you're yoked.

Strength is simple, but not easy. Your body doesn't get stronger on your schedule. You will have bad days or even bad weeks. Stay strong. Stay savage. Bad workouts aren't cause for you to reevaluate your training. If you want to look and be strong, you must grind away at the lifts I've mentioned until your numbers are where you want them.

Even after a decade of lifting, the iron is still teaching me lessons. The most recent is the absolute power of the walking lunge. Back pain forced me to sideline the squat and deadlift. After a month of lunging, I tested the squat again and had a 30lb PR. Remember, your goal is to make your personal bests your new work sets. Master a weight, then add more. A man who uses 315 for bench work sets looks far better than the man who can bench 315 one time.

Devotion, always devotion. Become intolerant to failure.

24.
CIMMERIAN NECK POWER

I believe bodybuilding is gateway drug back to nature. Training is necessary for all men. My own love of training goes beyond obsession — it's pure devotion. BUT I'm not a bodybuilder or a powerlifter. There's nothing wrong with training for sport, but the specialization required comes at great cost. Powerlifters struggle to go up stairs, bodybuilders don't have the power their body portrays. I'm fan of the Barbarian Aesthetic. Men must make themselves intimidating and hard to kill. Become a massive hulking barbarian! It's not enough to look the part, you must become power. You must train for strength AND aesthetics. You all know about Conan the Barbarian, right? This is what you should strive for.

Conan was big, but also as quick and nimble as a panther. The product of a hard life — the barbarian life.

Have you read *Shadows of Zamboula*? *Shadows of Zamboula* has Conan helping some woman — in hopes he'll get laid afterwards — but she's abducted. Conan while trying to get her back runs into the bad guy's henchmen, a brown acolyte named Baal-Pteor. This man was massive and used illusions to confuse the barbarian. Baal-Pteor taunts the Cimmerian, boasting he had been twisting heads off people since he was a child. He started with babies, then to children and women.

When he became an adult, he twisted the heads off men. All with his bare hands. This Baal-Pteor was a strangler. After discombobulating Conan, Baal-Pteor's hands closed around his neck for the kill. The barbarian didn't try to stop this.

Right after feeling the chords of muscles in Conan's neck, Baal-Pteor gasped as the Cimmerian's hands locked around his neck. They stood there in a battle wills — and necks. The veins in their temples begun to show. It was at this moment that Conan grinned at the acolyte. Fear shown in Baal-Pteor's eyes. Conan's thick neck would not give. Baal-Pteor started to panic. He heaved and struggled to get free. The barbarian's fingers ground deeper and deeper into his neck. Conan overpowered the large man, prying him onto a table and this is where he told the acolyte:

"'You fool!' he all but whispered. 'I think you never saw a man from the West before. Did you deem yourself strong, because you were able to twist the heads off civilized folk, poor weaklings with muscles like rotten string? Hell! Break the neck of a wild Cimmerian bull before you call yourself strong. I did that, before I was a full-grown man—like this!'" -Conan

You must read to know what happens next, but you can probably guess. Pretty boys train to look pretty. Fat boys train to be strong. You need both.

Train your neck.

I can guarantee almost no one trains their neck. Maybe if you're training MMA or boxing, but beyond that no one trains the neck. Why? It's boring that's why. No one wants to put on the boring neck harness when you could be benching or curling. These are the mirror muscles the females see — but so is the neck. A thick, striated neck is True Cimmerian Power.

Everyone knows about the neck harness. If you don't have one, there is cheap Everlast harness on Amazon. A simple weight plate can be be used for front neck raises, done for high reps. Don't ever try to max out on neck exercises. Start light with 5lbs and get 100 reps in as few sets as possible. You can also use wrestler bridges and neck planks. If these seem too dangerous, they are scalable. Try first with lifting body off ground with head and traps pinned to ground.

I recommend one neck exercise per workout. Use 4-6 sets. Treat as finisher exercise. Not only will you be harder to kill, but a stronger neck will help with exercises like the deadlift and the press. You don't realize how your neck has to work during a heavy press. If you played football, you'd have gotten a stinger at some point this. That is what it feels like to tweak your neck during the press. Always train your neck.

25.
ESOTERIC STRENGTH WISDOM

Starting Strength by Mark Rippetoe is best way for a beginner to get to his physical limits fast. Only thing I would change is adding Pull Ups and Dips at the end of each session to balance the lower body gains. The biggest mistake lifters make with Starting Strength is believing it's meant to be ran long term. No — you only run the program until you hit the wall. 3-6 months on SS is all you need.

To stay on Starting Strength any longer is sacrificing overall fitness for strength. No one, and I mean no one, wants to spend 10 minutes resting between sets. Even 5 minutes is pushing it. After you hit the wall, move to a different program in line with your goals.

Stop maxing out. I get it, I really do. You want to move big weight. There are too many problems with maxing out that aren't worth the price tag. The first and most obvious is you risk injury. Everyone by now has seen the video of the guy's chest ripping off the bones while he tries to incline bench 500lbs. Yeah, there's times where you're going to want to see what you can do, but this should happen a couple times a year tops. 99% of the time you should be focused on increasing the weight on your working sets. A man who benches 315 for his working sets will look better than the man who maxes out at 315.

Last year(2020), I recall maxing out twice. Once for a Press early in the year and again for a Back Squat during the summer. The second, less obvious downside to maxing out is demoralization. You can't lift more weight every time. This is the same reason why you don't spend too much time on Starting Strength. The more you fail, the more your confidence in the program takes a hit. The weight on the bar isn't the only thing that matters. How many times can you lift it? For how many sets? How fast can you lift the weight for a 10x5? How fast can you recover from set to set? The more you fail a lift, the closer you get to demoralization.

Anyone who's lifted for a minute knows the existential crisis that hits you after a bad workout. You start questioning what you're even living for. Are you on the wrong program? Do you need to change it up? Should you start cutting? Or should you bulk? When you're training for strength or say want to hit a certain weight, you must train well below your max. You must think of yourself as mastering a given weight before you move on. It's not enough to be able to lift the weight. You need to demonstrate control and mastery of it.

Can you control the weight? Can you rep it over many sets? 3 to 5 sets ain't enough to master a weight. You need at least 10. Use multiple means of progression to measure your mastery of the lift. Starting Strength uses one form of progression: linear. It only cares about the weight on the bar. Your muscles however, don't grow from workout to workout. Hence why the

Starting Strength wall exists. The weight on the bar isn't the only thing that matters. You can get stronger without adding weight to the bar. There's other things you can measure. You can:

- Increase the reps you can do at a weight
- Increase the number of sets
- Decrease the time rested
- Perfect your form and control the weight(don't let gravity help you)

There are so many ways to get stronger without adding weight to the bar. Good programs will use multiple means of progression. One of my favorite ways to improve the Press is something called Reverse Pyramid Training (RPT), which has you do your heaviest set first and subtract 10% of the weight from subsequent sets. The RPT program uses the weight the bar and the number of reps performed to progress. You work in rep ranges like 6-8 reps. When you can hit 8, up the weight. The more forms of progression you can add to your program, the longer you can run it.

Not all exercises are created equal. Certain exercises just make you stronger. A back squat will yield better gains and development over a leg press. This doesn't mean you skip the leg press, only that you put a heavier focus on the back squat. Don't major in the minors as they say. Being able to do your deads, squats, and presses along with your bodyweight movements like lunges, pull ups, and dips brings you POWER in addition to aesthetics. They should always be a part of a good program.

That's all for now.

Lift eternal jacked and tan.

PART V:

MEN AND WAR

26.
ALL GREAT THOUGHTS ARE CONCEIVED BY WALKING

"All great thoughts are conceived by walking." -Friedrich Nietzsche

You should walk more. Every day. Not only is it good for the body, but also the mind. I'm going to do something different with this post. The thoughts I have during the walk will be elaborated here. Today's thoughts dwelled on three topics. The first topic is victor's justice in relation to Nuremberg and the new western religion. The second is about being closer to the primitive and the last section is on neo-masculinity.

I. Victor's Justice

If you're born into the west, you're indoctrinated into the narrative of the victor. Victors consider themselves both heroes and victims. The biggest mythos of the current age is the Holocaust and how White Men massacred the Jews and how the Allies came together to stop them. The reality is the Holocaust came out of the Second World War — really the second European Civil War — and there's a large amount of people who still believe it was fought to save the Jews. The Jewish story of World War II didn't start until after the conflict ceased during the Nuremberg Trial the following year. The Holocaust is propaganda. What makes their suffering any more important than the suffering of all the European peoples during the war?

If you believe in the Holocaust, you don't know the whole story. You only know what the victors of that war want you to know. More than likely, you don't see how Germany was treated after World War I and how that treatment set the stage for the second. The people you see as the "good guys" set the stage for a man like Hitler to rise. Historians go out of their way to paint Hitler as the reincarnation of Satan. Hell — he is Satan to the modern leftist. What are the odds that Hitler wasn't the devil he's made out to be?

I'm currently reading *Hitler: Beyond Evil and Tyranny* by R.H.S. Stolfi which sets out to write a historical, more realistic, biography of Hitler without the straight ridiculous propaganda that most historians use when studying the man. Again, Hitler represents evil incarnate to modern-day leftists, but how much of this is just fantasy? A man doesn't rise to the head of a nation-state without having some of the qualities of greatness. I will write about this book as soon as I finish, but there are already two stories of Hitler from WWI worth touching on. The first is his heroism and humanity in WWI. He earned an Iron Cross First Class in the war, captured many enemy prisoners, as well as rescued a stray dog during the war(a dog later stolen from him while he was on a mission).

The second story speaks to those of us in touch with nature and The Gods. Hitler told a story in 1935 of a moment when he started to believe in God or The Gods or prescience. He was eating at night with his company when some voice in his head told him to move. Hitler listened to this voice and moved away from the group, some twenty yards away. A half hour later a shell hit where he was sitting before killing everyone around it. Was Hitler guided to safety by Wotan? I think so.

The purpose of all this isn't to come out as some Nazi sympathizer but to show how you're being mindfucked by this gay regime. Do you think the Holocaust was the only Holocaust in history? It was only the most recent. There's nothing special about the Holocaust. Millions upon millions of people died in the Second World War — what makes the Jews so important? What about the some ten million Russians liquidated by the Soviets before the start of the war? Why does no one create a museum for them?

There's argument to be made that the Germans were as much of victims as the Jews. Their suffering doesn't get acknowledged, however, because they were the big bad to the Allies. Do not fall for narratives. You must see the world through primitive eyes, eyes that still see the work of Zeus at play, as Heraclitus says. This Holocaust narrative is used to destroy us and our culture. It must be grounded into a pulp.

II. Be Closer to The Primitive

Liberal academia claims to be at the forefront of progressive thought. The lefties are the most educated and progressive people in history. They've successfully outsmarted our bigoted forefathers and their racist traditions. In reality, if leftists ever realize what their masters took for them, we would see a chimp out on a scale never seen before. Leftist indoctrination has successfully removed western man from nature and placed him in a mammy-security state. All the mental and physical ailments of our people are by design, to keep us enslaved to the masters who milk us for everything we're worth.

If you want to survive the Kali Yuga, the coming of the dark age, you have to be closer to the primitive. Primitive man understood the workings of nature in a way we've forgotten. We've come to a point in a time where men believe we've left nature behind. It's even our responsibility to take care of nature like a child would his elderly parent. The truth is men are animools. We're beasts, THE beasts. Nature is still very much a part of life and if you don't see it at play you will be crushed.

You have to remember what you are. Man is the apex predator. We've conquered the world. What did it take to do this? You have to realize the elite are now conquering us and they've done a fine job so far. Your only way around this is to remember what's in the blood. There is a reason the state controls academia. They have a vested interest in keeping your true history and culture in the shadows, to prevent the ultimate chimp out against their reign. It's only by becoming closer to the primitive, the workings of nature, that you can mount counterattack.

What does it mean to be closer to the primitive? It means you understand what it means to be human. You know history, especially the history of your people and what got you to the top of the food chain. Modern propaganda is so powerful it's destroying everything that's distinctly human and turning us into cows to be milked. Men and women have roles and jobs in our society conducive to the survival and excellence of the tribe, but globohomo has destroyed these pillars. Much of this is just common sense, but it's not so common anymore.

The family is the foundation of the society. There is a biological imperative for men and women to leave behind children on this earth before they die. How many of these empowered men and women are suffering from deep depression because they were tricked into believing that having kids was overrated? They are the ignoble ends of their bloodlines. 99.99% of them won't even be remembered for their deeds. The tribe was likely created to assure the survival of the children. A society that ignores this is doomed.

Men and women are different. You don't have to be a rocket scientist to see this, yet so many believe there's barely any difference at all. There's a reason men are built for war and women are built to have children. The sexes have different jobs. If you try to ignore your nature for too long, you'll lose yourself to the regime. There's much respect to be had in both roles and both roles are required if you want your people to survive and thrive in nature. There's a reason we see race even as the whole liberal establishment tells us not to.

It's not necessary to hate different races, but it's important to realize that the races are different — each governed by different customs and values. You're here today because of your race's culture. Lose the culture, lose the people. The most demoralizing experience in the west is generations of Whites being turned against their own culture and people, made to feel guilty for shit they took no part in. No time spent on the great works done by their people. Traditions and customs exist for a reason. There's more wisdom in your body than in the deepest philosophy as Nietzsche said.

Science has yet to discover what's in the blood. They've always known about autonomous actions of the body, for example, you don't have to think about breathing, but if you stop breathing you die. To what extent are we governed by thousands of years of eugenic development? There's enough collective history of the world to know what makes a people great. Why do some strive, and others remain stagnant? Hard times forge strong men. You have to seek out discomfort to keep you strong in a world that wants you weak. Do this for you, your friends, and your kids.

III. Neo-Masculinity is Gay

Now — I believe being manly is vital for a man, but do not take it to the level of say teaching men's studies in schools. The tranny security state, of course, would never allow that, but it's worth saying for emphasis. Many of these Neo-masculinity movements are borderline gay and this must be prevented at all costs. A poster a long time ago said something along the lines of "things masculine men don't do: try to act masculine, read about how to become more masculine, and tell people they're masculine." When you talk too much about masculinity, you lose what it means to be a man. Men have a role in society, if you thrive in that role, there's no need to have to talk about how manly you are.

I used to want to make a men's website to help foster manliness in men, but the ideas for it always sputtered out. It just felt gay and the reason it feels gay is because this is shit all men should understand. It should be built into the foundations of society — and it isn't. Any healthy culture would build masculinity into it because, without strong men, your people won't be around for a long time. Some cruder people will just crush society and kill or enslave everyone. At this point, however, the elite have abandoned their people. They believe that they can just replace us with third-worlders and so far it's working out in their favor.

Keep the neo-masculine movement at a safe distance, with a stick if necessary. The gurus may have good knowledge of masculinity but don't expect to count on them when the shit hits the fan. Most gurus are glorified grifters. They survive off your patronage. Do you think you can trust — let alone depend — on these neo-masculinity gurus? They'll do what they can to keep the business running. They won't be doing any fighting. It's important to become manly but in an authentic way.

Authentic manliness must take into account what the Romans called virtus. We get our word virtue from virtus, but the word itself was associated with what the Romans saw as manliness in their time: the martial virtues. Primitive men were expected to fight. They had to be able to hunt and secure food, as well as go to war. Nietzsche said the free man is a warrior. The warrior has the will to be responsible for himself. The well-being of himself and his family depends on his ability to achieve victory. This is true freedom, not the fake shit we think we have in America.

Your training should be geared towards making you a better warrior. The majority of the men recruited for special forces grew up hunting and fishing. RW bodybuilding is fun, but you should also be able to fend for yourself.

27.
TO BECOME HEROIC

There isn't a whole lot I remember about being a kid, but I had one overriding desire during those years I haven't forgotten: to be heroic. A soldier or fireman, something like that. Obviously, I couldn't get bitten by a radioactive spider or get some trans-steron-super-soldier serum. Of course, by the time I graduated high school, I didn't do either of those things. I went to college like most kids. What the hell happened? Did my balls fall off? Maybe.

It wasn't until a couple of years later when I had a good hard look at the mirror that I remembered my childhood desire and set into motion my own metamorphosis. What does it mean to be heroic? What does it mean to be a hero? There's no shortage of heroes in the mainstream media. Whether you want to be "embarrassed" by it or not, comic book heroes are like demigods were to the Greeks. It's easy to dismiss them as being a part of the problem in modern culture, but I believe they still have value.

The superheroes portrayed in Marvel and DC movies offer us remnants of western heroism. Disney managed to turn Marvel into a cash cow. This happened because they were fulfilling a need. There's a need for heroes in our culture because the outlook of our future is immensely bleak.

Psychological operations waged against western culture since at least 1933 have had their effect. The west is committing suicide and half of its people believe that's a good thing. If you're American — and I mean red-blooded American — you're not allowed to be proud of your culture. By red-blooded, I mean your ancestral line has been around before the Civil War. American culture is evil. America is built on "stolen land." This is propaganda made to make you hate your own people. Lefties are all about being tolerant of all people, even those who are actively against their ideology(religion of peace anyone?). They're tolerant of everybody, EXCEPT White Americans. What's even more demoralizing is lefties are primarily made up of White Americans. Granted, they've become demoralized in Soviet terms.

This long-winded sidetrack is meant to explain comic book superheroes. Comic book superheroes are manifestations of western heroism. Most on the right and the left enjoy them and were likely raised by them. What the left doesn't realize when they watch a superhero movie is they're cheering for fascist authoritarians as Jonathan Bowden put it. The writers try to mask this by having the villains be "literal Nazis." If you don't know, the Nazis are the modern Christian demons who wait for liberals underneath their beds at night.

When you think of superheroes, you're usually thinking of a tall, jacked, and noble White Man. Woke culture tries to remedy this by making remakes with POC superheroes, but they almost never do well because we instinctively don't buy the characters.

I don't believe my experience was anything but normal. Boys instinctively want to become heroic. They want to emulate men with strength, courage, and honor. They even understand the concept of the heroic sacrifice. These are traits ingrained in the blood and bone of men. It's what enabled men to rise to the top of the food chain. Heroism in its very essence is just primordial manliness. Heroism was the men who protected the perimeter. Who fought in the threshold against the forces of chaos. And who figured out how to help their people survive and win when all hope seemed lost.

Mankind was selected for these qualities. Boys are born instinctively wanting to fulfill them. Why do you think we send kids to school for 12+ years? To beat their instincts out of them. To hide and conceal what's in the blood. You don't go to school to be educated. You go to be indoctrinated. Remember this when it comes to your own children. It's your responsibility to show them the way. Don't depend on teachers to do it for you. Teachers are unknowingly contributing to the destruction of the west.

The real heroes are the men who protect the tribe from destruction or men who increase the fame of the tribe through conquest. Comic book superheroes may inspire heroism in boys. They might just create bodybuilders. They do possess remnants of what it means to be heroic in western terms. The real heroes, however, are the men who protect the borders of their tribe. Who goes out into the darkness. Real heroes are also the men who save their culture from subversion.

The leviathan manipulates our people into self-destruction. It turns our people degenerate and separates them from nature. Those who follow their instincts and join the military get sent halfway across the world to fight in police actions that don't matter. Imagine if our heroic men were actually here. Imagine if they weren't spent from fighting some meaningless police action. The leviathan's grip wouldn't be so deep. Remember this as you raise your own children.

I don't think there is a way to save the west. What I call for here is a return to Barbaric Vitalism. You must find or create for yourself a small, trusted tribe within this degenerate empire. Make yourself resistant to the leviathan's influence and forge a new culture for a new age. Barbaric Vitalism is Nietzschean. It's not about trying to save what's already lost. It's about finding a way or making one. To survive and THRIVE. It's about forging a new path and creating a new order. It's about winning.

Because that's what heroes do. (Lol)

28.
ARE SUPERHEROES A PSYOP?

James Lafond mentioned how the invention of superheroes destroyed the primordial concept of the hero. This is interesting to consider. Is the superhero another psyop in the war on men? Or were superheroes a product of their environments? Superman showed up on the scene in 1938. About a generation after the Great War. Perhaps, his creation was in response to the devastation of modern war. The greatness, power, and glory the men of WWI thought they were marching off for wasn't there. Many were to be the thirteenth charge against an entrenched enemy position to only pick up a few more yards. And they would be mowed down just like the twelve charges before them.

There was glory to be found, Ernst Jünger was an example of this, but for most men who thought they were about to show their manhood and heroism, the war was sobering. Superman being what he is seems to be a response to modern warfare. It is known that communists were at Franklin D Roosevelt's ear as early as 1933 and that Hollywood is not a form of entertainment, but propaganda. Superheroes could very well be a psyop designed to demoralize men into some realization that they could never be a hero because they didn't get the super soldier serum or weren't born on Krypton.

The men who came before had a different concept of the heroic. Their heroes were not web-slinging spiderman or a guy who builds a super iron suit for himself. They didn't imagine their heroes as being many times stronger than normal men. Jonathan Bowden believed superheroes were a form of psyop against men, but perhaps not in the same way Lafond sees them as a psyop. What Bowden saw in superheroes were men who possessed everything a fascist surfer bodybuilder would want.

Superheroes possessed the same values as authoritarian knuckle-draggers, but they were always made to fight for liberal causes. They were first made to look like the men they wanted to influence: White Americans. But these superheroes would fight for ideals that undermined the people who read and enjoyed them. This brings me to primordial heroism. The primordial hero wasn't meant to be something unattainable by the everyman. He was meant to inspire men toward greatness, power, and glory as well as teach us about human nature.

Primordial heroes were mortal men, though many thought that by being descendants of Gods, they were stronger than normal men. They weren't, however, invulnerable like Superman. Primordial heroes were consumed by righteous thumos to fight monsters to protect or champion their people. Heracles took on chthonic beasts to make the world safe for mankind. Achilles took on the Trojans and defeated Hector to avenge the death of Patroclus in the name of immortal fame. Both of these heroes were mighty and powerful but also suffered from being men. They had their vices whereas modern superheroes are made to be morally perfect.

Whatever the case of their origin, the superhero is corrupted now. There is no mistaking how far-gone superheroes have become. When and where it happened or if they were always meant to be subversive is up to debate. By all means, be a superhero movie enjoyer, but don't use the superhero as the basis of your manly framework. I can't get into superhero movies anymore or most movies for that matter. The social conditioning, the pathetic virtue signaling, and trying to create females who are as strong as males are all tiresome, boring, and unbelievable. It is quite the turnaround that I now find powerful value in the heroic epics.

This is a challenge to the uninitiated. Watch your most recent superhero movie. The one that makes sure to have a woman superhero with some bipoclgbt character make their virtue signals to forward their social justice programs and then, revisit a heroic epic like the *Iliad*. The contrasts are stark. If you read Apollodorus on Heracles, you find that he isn't anything like his boring Disney counterpart. *The Iliad* is more exciting than any action movie you can watch today. The short stories about Conan the Barbarian by Robert E Howard carry the spirit of the heroic epics. They too, should be read.

Recently, I started reading *Beowulf*. A man whose grip is as strong as thirty men tears the arm off the monster Grendel. He does combat with the monster unarmed, as the monster is unarmed. Man to man. There's belief this poem is blood memory from another time when men did battle with Neanderthals. Neanderthal were said to be covered in fur. Their strength was four times that of men and they could see in the dark. The monster Grendel would only attack at night. What if the Neanderthals represented the orc of the primordial world, the Norse jotun?

The primordial hero offers man the path to greatness, power, and glory. The superhero seeks to disarm and disprivilege. The primordial hero is a piece of human nature and his epic both gives courage to men and teaches us about the world. Manhood and heroism go hand in hand because it is men who fight monsters. What makes for a strong man, opens the possibility for heroism. Make no mistake, there are still monsters to be vanquished.

29.
HYPER-MASCULINITY

Before I begin, it's important to remember how few break the brainwashing. Most end up mindfucked for life. I was fortunate enough to be awakened in my early twenties after discovering the iron. It all started with a realization, the man in the mirror wasn't the man I thought I was. Many don't shake off the brainwashing and remain mindfucked. If they're lucky, maybe they find the neo-masculine sphere that isn't banned from the mainstream. But this is only temporary solution. Many in the neo-masculine sphere are still thralls to the system. Their knowledge aids but doesn't free the thrall mind.

Society's been waging a holy war against masculinity since before any of us were even born. You're raised in the ways of emasculation through school, taught to fear your inherent "toxic masculinity." Often the only one who will show you the solar path out of this modern hell is yourself, in sheer despair, trying to cope in the modern world. From there, it's about asking the right questions. Modern men are raised on superheroes, the idea of equality, and feminism, and to fear their instinct for otherwise, their toxic masculinity might rear its ugly head. When push comes to shove, not even this effeminate male wants to be known as a coward. He wants to be a hero, like that Captain Marvel chick — an ally to the oppressed.

All men start with the desire to become heroic. This is the first question young men will ask, often also related to getting laid. How can you become that guy? How can you be the man everyone looks to when the shit hits the fan? And God damn it, how can he get laid? One fortunate development of the technology age is the mass availability of information. The answers are there if you look for it. Granted in this day and age of centralization and censorship, it's harder to find. But it's still out there. This path typically ends with said man getting swept into the neo-masculine sphere. There are problems with this. Overall, the sphere is a net good for the war effort, but the messages are often idealistic and separated from nature. They're also way too connected to the conservative movement and often thrall to their values without realizing the leadership of this party is just as fucked up as their "opposition."

The superhero is in essence a psyop against the man, making the heroic seem impossible in this technological age. You have to be from krypton to stand a chance against the bullet or the drone high in the sky. Superheroes are demoralizing in nature because they plant the seed of heroism without offering the path to it. And then the young man falls back to the desire to get laid. Getting laid affirms his worth in a way, coupled with the desire to leave his mark on the world through having sons. This is all good and well, but these men aren't getting the path out of hell. The leviathan has already weaponized these desires against him.

The answer then, falls back on masculinity. How can you be good at being a man? This is the next step for the man if he continues on the journey. He realizes he can't be heroic without first becoming a man. Now, he must first navigate the difference between being a good man and being good at being a man. If he gets here, he's well on his way. The problem is when he figures out what it takes to be good at being a man. If you reach this point, your reality starts to shatter. You realize the world isn't what it appears to be. There's a fake world hiding the real one, like bloatware on a phone. As Heraclitus said, "Nature loves to hide."

The man who reaches this point must make a decision. See how far the rabbit hole goes or settle with just being good enough. A man at this stage knows how to deal with females, but is most likely still thrall to the system. For example, he's still a fan of sportsball, binge drinking, and the like. Yeah, politicians ARE cockroaches, but at least there are still honorable men out there in the military. Teachers do good work, and your doctor is working in your best interest. But the moment you decide to take this further, it becomes the itch you have to scratch. It's not about becoming heroic or figuring out how to be good at being a man, but determining what man is supposed to be in nature.

To become heroic, you must first become a man. To become a man, you have to figure out what man is in nature. Once you do this, you get introduced to nature. The very thing modern education tried to hide from you. You begin to see how power works in the real world and this knowledge breaks this fake reality we exist in. Natural Law or Might Makes Right becomes known to you. Or as a barbarian put it to the Romans after conquering Rome, "Vae Victus!" Woe to the vanquished.

Then you learn there is a pecking order to every group within nature. A pecking order of species, the food chain. Pecking order of nations. Hell, there's a pecking order to everything down to the smallest groups. If you want to compete in nature, you have to be a winner. And from there, it begins to get real. The subjects you believe didn't matter (because science!) or are taboo suddenly become relevant. What if you were lied to on a scale you couldn't even dream of? All this started with realizing you were being lied to about what it takes to get females and be good at being a man, how bad does it get?

Masculinity has gone down the road of boring. It's either bashed relentlessly by leftists or given this regal-like status by a conservative "opposition" that doesn't go far enough to bring about positive change or even recruit resistance. To effect real change, to light a fire in men's souls, you must appeal to vitality and nature. You have to see a man for what he is — a beast in nature. He's driven by a barbaric will to life that gets hidden from him through years of social indoctrination.

Depression in the young or later on, the midlife crisis, represents the man trying to reawaken his spirit to fight. He knows something is wrong.

Vitality can only be expressed through true manliness. Creating men who are not only massive and strong, but aware of the reality of nature. Who dares to face injustice with thumos. Only in this state can they go about trying to master space and the conditions they were born into which is the unconscious goal of every man.

Becoming manly gets you back to the original question of becoming heroic. You return back into the world with the power of Nemesis, to give what is due to the monsters who rule over us. The man in nature has within him the potential of the primordial heroes we don't talk about anymore. Of Heracles and Achilles and Odysseus. Of Beowulf and Gilgamesh. Romulus and Remus. Even Conan the Barbarian doesn't get his due, perhaps the last written primordial hero. To become heroic comes down to becoming manly in the true sense of the word. To reach a state all men dream of with the will to carry out your desires. To impose your will and leave your mark on the world.

30.
THE WARPATH

Modern men are raised in an anti-war environment. Make love, not war as the hippies say. There is some wisdom in this as modern warfare is devastating and there are no better reasons for the wars in our time. Ok, sir, I will go get blown up in Afghanistan or Iraq, two countries that pose zero threat to the United States. No, I can't recommend you do this. Police action wars are garbage. HOWEVER, men need war. Nietzsche in *Twilight of the Idols* says, "war trains men to be free."

The plight of modern men isn't death in war, but the absence of war, of struggle. Helicopter parents don't let their boys experience hardship. Schools snuff out bullying and hurt feelings. Rites of passages are all but non-existent. We're being raised to be good slaves for the new world order. The goal of ZOG is to make you meek and docile. They're not interested in the manly virtues that make the foundation of a tribe or civilization. Power and money are all they're after. A society of strong men is a threat. Perhaps, this is the reason many get tricked into joining military and are immediately shipped out to the Middle East.

The act of war forces man into action. There's nothing more liberating than the ability and will to fight. For ancient men, war is what made them free. They received everything from the spoils of war to their own freedom by fighting and winning. The Roman word virtus which became the word virtue in English meant manliness. The "vir" of virtus meant man. The Romans — when they spoke of virtus — meant valor, manliness, excellence, courage, character, and worth. Every male wasn't considered a man until they had displayed their physical power, energy, and vitality. The title of man had to be earned by proving your worth.

Back then, virtus was proven by physical prowess. Such a world doesn't exist anymore, but virtus is something that I consider part of the natural rites of men. It's been around much longer than the early Roman Republic. The Greeks had a word for it too: arete. When the Greeks thought about arete, they thought about Achilles. Virtus and arete were what it was called when you were good at being a man(notice I didn't say good man).

In the absence of war, you must create your own war. Cernovich today is just a grifter. He's found his market, and he wants to keep his market, but I believe his book *Gorilla Mindset* is not wrong. You can program your own mind like a computer. You can be happy, sad, or otherwise based on choice. When you learn this, the bad days will never hit as hard as they used to. That said, you must train yourself to wake up every day ready to go to war. And you have plenty to go to war over. Are you happy with your physique or strength? Are you a thrall to the empire? If you're not fit, if you're not war ready, when I say wake up ready to go to war, I mean get into the gym and fucking train like your life depends on it(it does).

Almost no one is where they want to be. The vast majority of us are thralls to the empire. Find something to sell or produce. To work for yourself is in part freedom. You don't have to worry about being fired from the words you say. Take any problem you're having in life and go on the warpath. Freedom must be taken. It'll never be given to you. Fight for your freedom every day. Always be on the warpath. And most importantly, remember: ONLY VICTORY.

31.
THOUGHTS ON WAR

"The life of man upon earth is warfare." Job 7:1

This will be controversial to normies, be careful! Men need war. They need to be on the warpath. The way modernity attacks war is detrimental to the male psyche. Every boy dreams of becoming the hero. They dream of getting their chance to face off against evil, against disorder, and chaos. Modernity hits the boy hard with every intent of destroying this dream and more. If you trace the evolution of men back to the base camp, the fire represents order, and the surrounding darkness is chaos. The first men who built the fire and watched the perimeter have always had different needs and passions compared to the women and children they protect.

The eyes of the first men are focused out into the darkness. They must look for encroaching threats during the night and resources during the day. The darkness was where they proved their worth to the tribe. What lay beyond the base camp? Honor and glory.

"But what about love and peace, brah?" Modernity preaches on end about the evils of war and yes, war is terrible. But in the prevalence of universal peace, men lose meaning. Suicide rates skyrocket in the absence of war. Men are driven into degeneracy precisely because they believe life to be meaningless. They embrace escapism through television, video games, and social media. To distract from facing the question of purpose.

War creates meaning. As Heraclitus says, "War is the father of all things." When there is no war, man finds himself in a void with no meaning or purpose. Without war, darkness and depression seep into your consciousness. The problem with modernity is this forced emphasis on "peace." Now, there isn't world peace. The oligarchs who rule over this understand the importance of war which is why the USA has been involved in endless police actions. It's a way of sending out what little virile fighting power we have left to foreign lands. This does many things for the elite. It removes males of fighting age who could be utilized to fight the elite class currently fucking over Americans.

These men who fight in these police actions, if they aren't killed or maimed, come back to America spent. After their experience, they aren't interested in fighting unless they absolutely have to. In a sense, their experience has pacified them. I mean these men no disrespect, they are heroes — but I believe their noble instincts have been misused by our crooked elite. Had these men not been shipped off to fight useless foreign wars, America would not be in the state it is end. They would not have allowed the oligarchs to get away with milking the country dry.

This not fed post. You should not expose yourself to fed goons trying to make you into the next Waco. There's nothing out there now that is effectively combating the rape of America. All that you can do for now is take care of you and your frens. Make preparations. Make yourself the barbarians who will become post-apocalyptic warlords in the age to come.

War is state of mind. Modernity makes everything seem hopeless. Everything is seemingly ok stacked against us. There's no clear path forward. It's just darkness and chaos. What can you do to stave off the darkness and hopelessness that's sending many men to take their own lives? What can you do to keep fighting and stave off the temptations of escapism?

You must go on the warpath. You must wake up every morning ready for war. War can be a state of mind. Going to war doesn't mean you have to go do something stupid, something that has little — if any — chance of success. The warpath is a mindset. Your war is against weakness. It's against anything that stands against your arete, your virtus. Your war is being fought for you — for your victory in life and your undying glory. Your enemies are the obstacles that stand before you. Whatever it is that's preventing you from reaching your goals. This requires thought about how you want your life to play out. What is your purpose? What do you want to do?

When you think like this, you have purpose. You're pursuing the Great Work. Your life has meaning because you're doing something other than just breathing and going with the flow. When you have purpose, you're very much in the game. You aren't going to be discouraged by things out of your control for your eyes are set on the prize, your end game.

Channeling the warpath is the essence of barbaric vitalism. It's having a Yes-to-Life Mentality. It's life-affirming. It's recognizing that despite all this comfort and technology, we're still very much a part of nature, and like the first men, our eyes are focused outwards into the darkness. It's from this darkness, this disorder where we'll forge our legacies and leave our mark on the world.

32.
HEROIC VISIONS FROM WORLD WAR I

I've always been fascinated with World War I. The conflict completely changed how the world — and the men within it — saw war. It was the convergence of hero worship and modern warfare. Up to this point, men yearned for war as an event that would allow them to show their heroism and defend their country. Men marched into WWI after greatness, power, and glory. Their sentiment is still around but to lesser degrees. We know WWI for what it was: a wide-scale slaughter of perhaps our last generation of real men. Armies went into this war holding idealisms that had to die if they were to win — and they didn't realize this until much later.

The sheer devastation imposed upon men would push them to their limits and beyond. It caused shell shock, and it was punishable by death because the officers of that time saw it as cowardice. These men were cowards to them. The science of PTSD wasn't there yet, it was only developed because of what happened during WWI. The generals — on both sides — believed during the first years that the way to win the war was to just throw more men at the enemy. There are days — yes, days — where a single country would report tens of thousands dead. This meat grinder didn't stop when the trenches were dug either. Men would have to watch advance after advance get mowed down by machine guns, dozens of times, then be expected to go out over the top themselves when their name was called.

How many men would you send over the trench to be slaughtered before you said enough, we have to figure something else out? Would you do your duty — to die pointlessly — after watching hundreds die before you, all for nothing? There was no heroism in this, but the men of WWI did their duty because they didn't know any better. As I said, this was the convergence of hero worship with modern warfare. The French wore the same uniforms they did when we were led by Napoleon a hundred years before. The men on all sides were made of something we can't even fathom today. Their constitution was strong. Think strength, courage, honor, and loyalty on steroids and you might get close to the character of these men. But the Great War even broke many of them. Hell, I'd bet most of the men who were executed for cowardice were more men than any of us living today.

Modern history puts so much interest into the Second World War and evil Nazis boogeymen. It's my opinion that we should be honoring the men of WWI far more than we speak about the Holocaust. The immortalization of the Holocaust is a product of psychological indoctrination. The aftermath left men embracing weakness and blaming themselves for something someone else did. The men of WWI were heroes of the highest order. They walked into hell. Imagine Mordor from *Lord of the Rings*, this is what WWI soldiers saw. Tolkien himself fought in WWI, so it's not hard to see how some of what he wrote was based on his experiences there. Imagine taking cover in a shell hole as the land is blown to kingdom come with artillery. Around you are bodies of soldiers. Some your own, others so badly decomposed you have no idea who they are.

There was no picking up your dead. In the trenches, you would live with the corpses of soldiers who died before you — sometimes years before you. In Paschendale, soldiers would fall into mud pits and drown because no one could pull them out. Others were caught unaware from their trenches as plumes of smoke billowed into them. These men would be the first to die from poison gas. Despite this, WWI soldiers showed absolute valor and devotion to country. There are stories of men going over the top to save wounded men who cried out. Going over the top was entering what was called No Man's Land. There was no cover, and you became easy pickings for the other side. The Germans, even though they surrendered, were never pushed back behind their borders.

How it must have felt to lose the war despite never being pushed back into Germany. To make it worse, they were utterly condemned and humiliated for the war. This treatment of Germany after WWI was the reason for Hitler's rise before WWII. The soldiers of WWI held strong constitutions that were reinforced by the knowledge of natural law. When they volunteered for service, they sought adventure and to protect their country. But beyond this, they were after greatness, power, and glory. They were men of strength, courage, honor, and loyalty.

Every account I've read from WWI veterans depicted men who cared about honor. They didn't hate their enemies, by contrast, they had great respect for them. This is something like inconceivable to a generation raised to despise the evil Nazis. The men of WWI existed on a different level. They admired the valor of their enemies. I speak of this because, in the current climate, psychological conditioning makes us hate our enemies with the ultimate ire. Leftists want the right wiped from the earth, their monuments broken, and their institutions destroyed. There is no respect, only hatred. This can only exist in a culture not raised by natural law.

I encourage you to read about WWI. Dan Carlin has an amazing 6 part podcast on the Great War. Of course, don't forget about Ernst Jünger's *Storm of Steel*. Also, read Alan Seeger's poem *I Have a Rendezvous With Death* which he wrote just before he died in WWI. You must absorb the character and constitution of these men, and recreate it in this degenerate age. You too must have heroic visions and embark on the solar path.

33.
A HERO'S DEATH

The *Epic of Gilgamesh* is the earliest recorded heroic saga. Put down to tablet in the cradle of civilization, Mesopotamia. It tells of the tyrannical, yet mighty King, Gilgamesh. He wasn't like other men, being two-thirds divine, he had legs that were nine feet long and muscle-like rock. There's a certain power that comes with the ancient, heroic saga. They offer a taste of real human nature. Not the fantasy crap we get in modern culture and superheroes. They also reveal what it means to be heroic, to be a man in nature, as well as offer us glimpses of a forgotten primeval world.

The massive king had nine-foot-long legs. Is he some man-giant hybrid? Is his eternal fren, Enkidu, half Neanderthal? Also, the epic speaks of a flood like the biblical flood. Did the Christians get the idea of the flood from the Sumerians?

Modern culture is filled with weak men afraid of death. "Men" are stacking vaccines to save themselves from wuhan flu like Rich Piana stacked his sheer natural talent to build muscle. They're so afraid of dying alone in a hospital they've forsaken life entirely. Now — I too, don't want to die in the longhouse, but like a man with an ounce of common sense, I choose to trust in tried-and-true ways of fighting disease. Sun and steel.

Early on in *Gilgamesh*, the king makes a powerful call to action to his fren Enkidu to go with him to slay the Guardian of the Cedar Forest, Humbaba the Terrible. Gilgamesh understands his mortality and he wants to leave his mark on the world by vanquishing the monster. Enkidu however, wants no part in this quest, believing they won't succeed. Gilgamesh — through sheer strength of will — convinces Enkidu to join him. They travel to the forest, a journey taking six days. Each night, a ritual to their victory is performed by Enkidu and each night Gilgamesh awakens in terror from a vision. Enkidu interprets each nightmare vision as a sign leading to their victory.

When they finally reach the forest, Enkidu loses his resolve and wants to return to their city in shame as a coward. Gilgamesh talks him through it, but he too almost falters at the entrance to Humbaba's den. This time Enkidu talks him through the fear, and they face the guardian together. This part of the epic perfectly depicts the human condition. How often do men talk tough before a fight, only to encounter terrible fear before the battle, to find themselves face to face with cowardice? In the *Iliad*, warlords spent much time coaxing their men to action by appealing to their honor by questioning their courage.

No man wants to be called a coward. Like true frens, Gilgamesh and Enkidu protect each other's honor. Their tale, however, isn't like the superhero movies we've grown accustomed to. The soy mind wouldn't be able to appreciate this epic.

Part of the power of the *Epic of Gilgamesh* is the journey of Gilgamesh. The hero's journey is well known, but the journey of Gilgamesh though it shares some similarities does not offer any satisfaction. I would argue however, it coincides with the pursuit of the Great Work. Most men aren't acquainted with death. They think they'll live forever. There's no attention spent on how they'll leave their mark on the world. It's just mindless comfort-seeking degeneracy. This is what makes Gilgamesh's strong desire to face Humbaba so powerful in the modern age.

It's not that Humbaba is some threat to Uruk, Gilgamesh's kingdom. He's not terrorizing the city's inhabitants like Grendel in Beowulf. He's the Guardian of the Cedar Forest. This is purely Gilgamesh seeking immortal glory. He wants some way to leave his legacy behind, to be remembered. This ninnie society would scoff at this, but ancient heroes would understand the emotions of Gilgamesh in the blood.

Gilgamesh is far from the superhero archetype. In the beginning, he's a tyrant king who puts the men under him into indentured servitude and lays claim to the virginity of all the females under his rule. He does, however, become a benevolent king by the end of the epic. His journey to find eternal life is striking. Unlike Heracles who is purified and made into a God at death, everlasting life is denied to Gilgamesh by The Gods. He meets the last man to be made immortal at the edge of the world, Utnapishtim, who survived the great flood that wiped out mankind.

This immortal gives Gilgamesh a chance to become a God. But to do this he must stay awake for seven days. Gilgamesh fails terribly. He must return to Uruk ragged, old, and mortal, but his epic, however...

34.
MAN AS BEAST

One notion of living in the modern world that's been forgotten by men is the notion of man as beast in nature. Man as beast is something inconceivable to us. Men are supposed to be above nature now. We're the guardians of nature, charged with its continued survival. The Greeks knew better. Homer's *Iliad* stands apart from all other ancient and religious texts in this respect.

The Iliad stands as the best text to study if you want to know about human nature and man as beast in nature. Modernity and leftist thought has done a number on our psyche to convince us that somehow men conquered nature — we're on a different path now. This mode of thought must be crushed. If you don't understand human nature and the natural order, you're doomed to the slaughterhouse as a nobody. No one will remember your name. You'll do nothing of worth. I can't understate this enough.

What makes *The Iliad* so powerful is it gives a fair account of human nature. Homer presents men as men, not some infallible Gods or goodly superheroes. For every powerful act a hero does in the book, Homer relates it to nature, from something he witnessed. The Greeks identified they were just as part of nature as any lion or any sheep. Like any beast in nature, they were trying to survive and the great texts they passed on from generation to generation were meant to tell their youth what qualities they needed to develop to become strong. These were qualities valued by the Ancient Greeks.

The Iliad showed how heroes strived for honor and did everything possible to avoid shame. The warlords of the armies constantly questioned their men's resolve — to keep the desire to flee at bay. It took a heroic man to stand strong in a shield wall. The pull of cowardice was always there and in ancient warfare, terror induced routs. Honor and shame were what motivated men to do great things. The Greeks weren't a guilt-based culture like we are today. The guilt didn't come until after Christianity.

Man as beast is something you must return to. The resavaging of men to their primal selves is the most important issue of our time. (Yes, not identity politics.) The longer you buy into the lie of modernity, the more risk you put yourself into in the future. The Ancient Greeks saw city-states come and go like the seasons. They had to foster in their men the virtues that would help them survive. Strength, courage, and honor were all necessary. Man as beast helped the Greeks see mankind's terrible qualities. To prepare them for life. *The Iliad* is full of gore, but not just gore. Each time a hero was slain, there was a fight for his armor. They looted the bodies right on the battlefield. Not only that, but they would also mutilate the deceased if they had caused them some kind of offense.

More, you get to learn the real differences between the sexes. The conquered women were taken into the enemy camp as slaves and would-be wives. You hear about the story of Briseis, who was captured by Achilles before the start of *The Iliad*. As she mourns the death of Patroclus, you find out that Patroclus comforted her as Achilles killed her husband and promised her Achilles' hand in marriage afterward. Yes, that's right. The real world is not a nice place. The women of conquered peoples were often taken by the conquerors.

In nature, man is stronger than woman. It's only laws that make us equal. But it's better to see men and women as compliments to each other. While men were stronger, their lives meant less than a woman's. This is why the men, the old, and the children of conquered people were often killed, but the women were taken into the enemy tribe. Women are the key to a tribe's future. No children equal no future. A man is just nature's plaything, entirely expendable. I encourage everywhere to read the *Iliad*. It's your best-unbiased chance at getting a look at real human nature.

It's not unbiased in that these were the real accounts of what happened at Troy, no, these were the virtues of the ancient Greeks. What Homer was trying to do was instill the right virtues into future generations so they would survive as his own did. Again, during these times city-states came and went like the seasons. Some were conquered, others died for other reasons. These virtues as said by Homer were what they believed necessary to survive in nature.

Maybe the actions of these heroes weren't based in reality, maybe they were. You still get the best account of life during the Bronze Age as well as the virtues the people of the time found important. Take the time to understand the *Iliad* and you'll get a better idea of how to get ahead in life. Anyone curious about human nature must read Homer.

35.
ROMAN ANIMUS

Manliness peaked in the Ancient Roman Republic. I believe any serious study of manhood will prove this. So, if you're going to study what made the Romans the most manly, you must start with their soul. Romans had a different conception of the soul than we do. They called it the animus. When I think of the word animus, I think something along the lines of "animal spirit." This may not be far from the mark.

In layman's terms, for the Roman to prove himself a man, he had to prove his worth through the demonstration of his will, his animus. In modern times, we know little about Roman culture. And hell, what we think we know about them is mostly wrong. Modern institutions teach that the Romans had this great, massive empire that eventually fell. It was this empire which the early colonial Americans modeled the United States. The colonists, however, had a better understanding of Romans than we do today. It's an understatement how unknowledgeable we've become.

Most believe that because the Romans forged this great empire, they won most of their battles. No — they actually lost most of their battles. They were the Rocky Balboa of the ancient world. Their enemies were always bigger, stronger, scarier. The Romans however, demonstrated the superiority of their will and imposed it on their enemies.

The Roman Empire started first as a small republic. They hadn't yet conquered most of the known world and so the society itself was homogeneous. They didn't have the concept of guilt. Their society was built instead on the feelings of shame. It wasn't God or The Gods watching them, but their peers. They didn't worry about committing sins or being immoral so much as their worth to fellow Romans. They wanted to show the strength of their animus.

The animus was the expression of their will. It was their energy, vigor, and vitality. The word inertia comes from Latin. To us, it just means inaction, but to the Romans, it meant something more. They saw inertia as cowardice. The Roman spirit was always supposed to be moving. Roman legions, for example, would march all day and overnight they would build forts which meant not only did they carry their armor and weapons, but also their tools and supplies. Labor in the Herculean sense was important to them. Labor was the act of proving the strength of their will. When you learn about Roman culture, it's no surprise they held Hercules in high regard.

While they did have leisure, it was often used to reflect on the direction they wanted to focus their energy. The Romans were accountable to each other. The choice to be lazy meant all the eyes would be on you. This sense of honor and shame was at every level of Roman society from the centurion to the slave.

When you learn how the Romans lost most of their battles, yet still conquered the ancient world, you have to wonder how. Much of this had to do with their animus. It didn't matter how many legions were lost or defeated; the Romans would just send another. They had what marines would recognize as a death-before-dishonor mentality. They would rather die than supplicate to an enemy.

In these modern times, there's a lot of inertia. The Romans would think us all cowards. They believed in action. You had to perform labors to demonstrate your will and prove your worth. This is good mentality to have. Always push your limits. Comfort is cowardice. Better still, find men to help keep you and each other accountable. Geoffroi de Charny said, "*He who does more is worth more.*" Your will is your energy. Most people these days don't cultivate energy. They eat shit diets and don't train their bodies. To do more, you have to treat your body better. Eat and train like a man. And then, make use of that extra energy to leave your mark on the world.

Manliness isn't just about being strong and courageous. It's also about power and vitality. It's only through a powerful animus that you can demonstrate your worth.

36.
WHAT MAKES MAN

The manosphere was perhaps the movement that broke open this fake fantasy world the leviathan was crafting for our eternal enslavement. Now maybe you don't agree with this, but I'm reminded of classical musics professor I had in college indoctrination classes who made powerful claim that 99.9% of musics is made about love.

What brought many men to the manosphere is the strong instinct to continue their bloodline. Even if having sons wasn't on their minds, what's in the blood drives them to this end. And when you take on this journey, you get more than you bargained for. You realize all the authority figures in your life are lying to you. Women don't want a "nice guy." What women tell you they want vs what they actually go for are two different things. Once you come to this truth, the next question often is: "What else are they lying about?"

In some way, however, the manosphere is cringe or maybe it became so over time. The men in this sphere began to realize it was "inner game" that mattered. When you start to dive into the concept of inner game, you move into the niche of Neo-masculinity. Neo-Masculinity is our modern generation of males rediscovering what it means to be a man. There is nothing inherently wrong with Neo-Masculinity. Every man should be trying to increase his innate manliness. The problem is with the "gurus" that emerge in this sphere.

These gurus I don't want to spend a lot of time on these because this isn't focus of discourse. They spend much time speaking about the manly virtues but when push comes to shove, they're at best tourists and at worst, grifters. You must understand that while most men on our side want to change society to something closer to nature, these gurus profit off modern society. Their messages will sound dissident, but the substance isn't there. They'll refuse to touch on certain subjects, not so much because they think it doesn't matter. I think they do believe it matters, but they don't want to put the grift at risk. Their efforts are spent more on what I see as the byproducts of manliness, not what makes manliness.

They play into the idea that we're at the end of history. Race doesn't matter. Bloodlines and blood memories don't matter. All you have to do is max out your strength, courage, and honor to be manly.

Less talked about by these "gurus" is the big picture. You can paint lipstick on a pig, but it's still a pig. How many untrained big guys get smashed by little BJJ guys? How many courageous men get talked into traps by glowies? These "virtues" give the appearance of manliness, not actual manliness.

To grasp what makes a man, you have to first understand nature. One aspect of manliness these gurus talk about is the ability of man to go to war. Men are built for war. War is to man what giving birth is to woman. Now this doesn't mean there must be a perpetual war to satisfy the purpose of men, but going to war itself is a mindset man can master and adapt to his circumstances. The purpose of going to war is to protect, provide, and in a certain sense, master one's conditions. Mastering space is a desire all men have. Many bottle it down because they believe such desires to be taboo in a "modern society." And this is unto their ruin.

Imposing your will is another aspect of manliness little talked about by these "gurus." When you hunt, when you fight another man, your success depends on your ability to break the will of your enemy. You have to manifest a killer instinct, a will to win. The ability to die a hero's death over withering away into old age. To do this, you must possess powerful connection to your tribe. To know that your death preserves those you care about and your courage to face this end will be honored by them. Those trying to tell you that blood doesn't matter are trying to disconnect you from your manly instincts.

What's in the blood matters. Men have been around a long time. Our ancestors selected certain genes. There are blood memories that our "smartest" scientists have no grasp of. The instinct isn't given the respect it deserves.

Race is quick to be discounted by neo-masculinity gurus. They try to latch into the leftist framework that race doesn't matter, but there are many races and tribes throughout the world. Each adapted to different circumstances and practiced different rites and customs. You must be conscious of your own racial identity as well as the racial identities of those around you lest you find yourself in the situation facing Americans today.

Leftists would have you believe that caring about race automatically grants you membership to the Ku Klux Klan and

113

the National Socialist Party. Your race matters because it's a part of your bloodline. Your blood tells a story. Why were you born in California, Texas, or Virginia? How'd your people get there? It's something every man must discover for himself. The leviathan wants you to hide from your history for a reason. They want to plump you up like a cow and milk you for everything you're worth. Your bloodline is something they can't take from you. It makes you who you are.

When it comes down to it, virtues like strength and courage are by-products of your ability to impose your will and master space. They don't make the man. You must do the things that make your will strong and help you crush the wills of your enemies. This is manliness.

37.
MAKING THE MAN

Inside the boy is the makings of the man. It's in his blood. What do boys — unhindered by the demonic nature of modern parents — gravitate towards? A mother told my wife that her son had a natural liking for cars, trucks, tractors, and the like. It wasn't something she taught him to like, it came to him naturally. She said this with much surprise as our society's social conditioning runs deep. I imagine for her, she expected some like in cars or superheroes to be something imposed on the boy by a misogynistic culture, not something he would go toward on his own.

No, it's quite the opposite of that. Only the boy who's been attacked psychologically by the parents shows that kind of abnormal behavior. Boys come out of the womb understanding nature better than their modern parents who have been brainwashed for most of their lives. The attack on the phrase "boys will be boys" is an attack on nature. This phrase which has recently come under attack is part of a psychological campaign against men. Rome conquered the barbarians through a stratagem called divide and conquer. The American masters use the same stratagem against their own people as means of controlling the population.

In biology, you learn we have certain autonomous actions that our bodies do without having to think about. You don't think about putting one foot in front of the other as you walk, you don't have to think about breathing. Your body does it on its own so you can use your brain on other matters. Scientists likely underestimate the body's autonomy. Or perhaps, the true extent of it is hidden from us. A boy knows in his blood what it means to be a man. Most men as children fantasized about being a powerful hero who gets the girl at the end. They want to be firefighters and soldiers because they know in the blood what their job is.

The purpose of education is to destroy what's in the blood. To convince the boy he is wrong to believe what he does. This is the true tragedy of being born in this age. So many are led on, believing they're learning about "progress," when it's just a charlatan's way of keeping you a thrall. If you're a father, prevent the institutions from brainwashing your son and if you're a boy, trust your instincts. Your mind understands things it cannot explain to your brain. You don't have to be able to rationalize an instinct. Just act on it. What the school system does is introduce you to fear without the teachings of courage.

If you want to become great, you will have to take risks. Our society only succeeds by paralyzing you with fear. The boy knows in the blood he has to take risks, which is why many go through phases best described as fearlessness. They want to prove their worth, but modern culture doesn't afford them their rite of passage into manhood. Many cultures had initiations for their boys. Where the boy would pass into the threshold, experience hardship, and emerge a man. The Romans for example, distinguished between males and men. A man was something you had to become. The Spartans took their boys from their mothers at age 7 to begin training.

In America today, and most of the world, boys just become "men" over time. This is not ideal. Some might realize their inadequacy and make moves to reverse it. This is good, but how much better could this man have been had there been someone to guide him? And what of the "men" who never really become men? Just perpetual boys, brainwashed by the system.

You want to know what makes a man? The man understands nature. He can separate nature from society. Society is designed to hide nature from the people, to allow the elite of society to garner more power and wealth at the expense of society. When you have power, the goal is to hold onto it and strive for more. The game was always rigged. The man can see the workings of nature in society. He knows might makes right. He understands that all things are organized in pecking orders. Most importantly, he understands that nature is never fair and will never be fair.

The man understands that no matter how many laws are there to "protect us," it is still his responsibility to protect himself and his family. And because of this, much of what makes a man is his ability to fight. Men are made for war. What war in the history of mankind was fought primarily by women? This is not attack on women. Women are built differently for different ends. Their roles are just as meaningful and honorable as the man's. We are compliments to each other. The problem a degenerating culture has is when too many people in the culture try to play opposite roles.

The Greek philosopher Heraclitus tells us, "*War is the father of all and the king of all; some he has shown to be gods and others men, some as slaves and some as free.*" The boy in nature has a strong desire to fight. To become a man, the boy must be trained in war. Perhaps, he will never see war, but he must be capable of it if he is to be a man. This idea alone would horrify the nanny state we live in where progressives try valiantly to create an everlasting utopia of peace. But the road to hell is paved with good intentions.

What makes a man is his ability to understand nature and master space. As boys, we're brought into this world and subconsciously driven to conquer the conditions we're brought into. Man has to be able to deal with the reality of nature in a way modern is incapable of. He knows what no one is willing to say aloud: the God and Creator of nature only cares about who wins.

38.
THE LAST LETTER TO HER SON, ANDREW JACKSON

I've been digging into *American Lion* by Jon Meacham, a biography about Andrew Jackson and was struck my the last letter he received from his mother, Elizabeth Jackson before she died when he was only 14 years old during the American Revolution.

Maybe you read and spread this power and wisdom to your sons?

"Andrew, if I should not see you again, I wish you to remember and treasure up some things I have already said to you; in this world, you will have to make your own way. To do that you must have friends. You can make friends by being honest and you can keep them by being steadfast. You must keep in mind that friends worth having will, in the long run, expect as much from you as they give to you.

To forget an obligation or to be ungrateful for a kindness is a base crime - not merely a fault or a sin but an actual crime. Men guilty of it sooner or later must suffer the penalty.

In personal conduct, be always polite but never obsequious. None will respect you more than you respect yourself.

Avoid quarrels as long as you can without yielding to imposition. But sustain your manhood always. Never bring a suit in law for assault and battery or for defamation. The law offers no remedy for such outrages that can satisfy the feelings of a true man.

Never wound the feelings of others. Never brook wanton outrage upon your own feelings. If ever you have to vindicate your feelings or defend your honor, do it calmly. If angry at first, wait till your wrath cools before you proceed."

39.
THE GREAT WORK

The concept of the Great Work is the missing link in talks about manliness. We live in a society that smothers exceptionalism. Most people don't have the faintest idea what their purpose is in the world and the elite capitalize on this. "What is the meaning of life?" is a question thrown around a lot. You have zoomers wishing death on themselves to avoid the quagmire of modern life. The meaning of life is easy: pursue the Great Work. Leave your mark on the world. Turn the wheel of mankind. What do you want to be remembered for? Meaning comes from purity of purpose.

The lack of purpose, of devotion to a cause, is perhaps the origin of everything wrong in society. It's how we've got to the point where there are 38 genders and we're being taxed to a point that would horrify the Founding Fathers. It's the reason weak minds are seduced by Marxism — so they don't have to figure out the meaning of life. They don't have to learn how to thrive, just suck the tit of big "brother." Of course, this way has many second-order consequences they didn't think about.

Lack of purpose encourages self-destructive behaviors in men. Whether you realize it or not, men are social animals. The feeling that you're not contributing to your tribe will send a signal to your brain that you're worthless. This signal sends you down the path of self-destruction. If you're interested in the interconnectedness of mankind, I recommend the book *The Global Brain* by Howard Bloom. In this book, Bloom talks about how mankind is connected. Many who believe themselves worthless to society end up taking their own lives. Inhumane studies on animals have shown that when you remove the comfort received from a mother to her child, the child will eventually die. This, too, is discussed in the book. These child animals would begin self-destructive behaviors before dying even though they were fed. The lack of affection ended them.

Men manifest similar self-destructive behaviors but rarely recognize the cause. Men will become depressed, eat more or less, and get addicted to drugs. They will isolate themselves from their people out of an incorrect instinct that they're a harm to their tribe. This dark road ultimately ends in suicide. The reality — if you find yourself in a similar situation — is that it's a product of your mind. It's not that you can't adapt, but you won't. In addition, you lack purpose. A man with purpose cannot be depressed so long as he remains in pursuit of the Great Work. Isolation is dangerous.

Most red-blooded Americans believe in rugged individualism. The frontier made us who we are. Bear in mind, however, that frontiersmen were pursuing the Great Work. That same path is not available to us anymore. Unless you're seeking to reforge a strong society in the flyover regions. Being cooped up at home with no friends or purpose is a death sentence. There is power in having frens. The community is important to your health. More specifically, a community focused on ascendence, on growth. Getting involved in a gym where everyone is focused on getting better or learning to fight is one of the best things you can do for yourself today.

The Great Work is the meaning of life. You don't get to choose how you come into the world, only how you leave it. Getting mad about oppression or injustice isn't conducive to a meaningful life. Your parents fucked you into existence. That is why you're alive. What most people want is a highly philosophical reason for existence. It either doesn't exist or it's beyond our understanding. You must make your own reason.

If you look at life from the perspective of nature, there are two means of pursuing the Great Work. I mentioned the book *The Global Brain* because the first means of "pursuing the Great Work" is simply having children. It's a biological imperative that everyone feels. Hidden in your blood is the will to reproduce. This is a way to leave your mark. If you don't get the job done, perhaps your offspring will.

Not having children is a form of isolation that can lead you down a dark road. Many will argue the world is too ugly or dangerous to have kids. This is a cop-out. If you're alive today, you've had ancestors who lived at the same time as the Black Plague, the fall of Rome, World War I and II. They somehow made it long enough to give birth to your forefathers. You owe your blood the same. The second means of pursuing the Great Work is the Golden Path. It's living fully the life of ascension. Your conquering eyes are set on the heavens, to leave your mark on the world in such a way mankind cannot forget you. This path requires you to become great.

If you can turn the wheel of mankind, you won't be forgotten. Few do this. Most will fail. This should not discourage you. Even if you fail in the pursuit, at least you have heart and a strong will. Your actions may influence even greater men to take up your sword. Always chase greatness. Make the Great Work your meaning to life. If you don't yet know what you want your Great Work to be, I recommend physical culture. Pumping iron or venturing into nature is great way to reconnect with what's in your blood. It is there you will find purpose. Don't believe the hype about strength and smarts being separate. The two feed off each other.

40.
THE DOMINATE PRIMORDIAL BEAST

I wrote once already about Jack London's *The Call of The Wild*, but it deserves a second look. *The Call of The Wild* is about a sled dog named Buck. I've known of the book for some time. It's always gotten good reviews. It was manly and primitive. But it took me a while to give it a chance — because it's about a dog. How could a book about a dog be a powerfuk example of manliness and nature?

This is a book about a dog returning to nature. Buck was the dog of some aristocrat in the Santa Clara Valley who was torn from his regal existence and forced to learn the "law of club and fang." Buck is trained to be a sled dog. A sled dog who was about to be made to travel through the Canadian winter. It's this experience in the wild that awakened in Buck the dormant dominant primordial beast. He was a house dog who was pulled from his home and was forced to become wild.

Buck finds himself in a power struggle with the other sled dogs, vying for that top spot in front of the sled. His story is very Nietzschean. It's as if he's read *Thus Spoke Zarathustra* and concluded that dog is something that must be surpassed. Buck is drawn to the primordial desire for greatness, to become master of his conditions. To conquer space. The experience of Buck is the experience of the modern man in his attempt to return to nature. When you start to see the world for what it is, when you start seeing nature at play, your worldview is forced to change. The mainstream morality all men in the West are raised on must die because that morality is the means of your enslavement. Nature doesn't care about your morality. Nature only cares about who wins, who is the best.

The Call of The Wild lays out the path for all men who want to escape the degeneration of the modern world. Buck, first living his comfortable life, is completely caught by surprise when he's taken from the place he considered himself king of. He's cruelly beaten, and forced to work, his food is stolen by his comrades, and conditioned to pull the sled. He loses some forty pounds on the journey but grows into a fearsome dog of power. Throughout this journey, Buck is still a slave with a master as it is with all men. But his job teaches him about the primitive, about nature. He is reconnected with his ancestors out there in the wilderness.

Buck's path was perilous. There was no mercy under the law of club and fang. The sled was vulnerable to all kinds of danger. To be thrown to the ground in a scuffle with another dog meant death, it meant the pack would turn on him. In addition, they worked in subzero cold and snow and ice. Over time his masters would change, some good, some fair, and some cruel. Like us, he was at the mercy of the master. The right master made him stronger, and the wrong master ran him into the ground.

You're a fool to believe yourself free in this alleged "Land of the Free." The laws and the customs are chains. Bonds to hold you down while men who understand the primitive law take advantage. This is no excuse to give in. To cry foul. This is simply how the world is. It's your duty to overcome. This is what Nietzsche called for when he said, "Man is something to be surpassed." You're born into a great game, a game hidden from you intentionally by your masters. To get a taste of the primordial is to destroy whatever worldview you might have had. To master your conditions, to conquer space. This is what you were made for, whether your parents realized it or not. Modern ailments such as depression are born out of this desire. You're meant to become the "dominant primordial beast" as London coined it.

You'll never be content otherwise. This is your Great Work. If it's not pursued, you will never have peace. Buck came out of a comfortable house, the house of an aristocrat. He thought he was a king. It wasn't until he got a taste of the wild that he realized how wrong he was. The call of the wild pulled him back to nature. To be what he was meant to be.

41.
ALL GREAT THOUGHTS ARE CONCEIVED BY WALKING II

When was the last time you took a walk? When was the last time you went out into nature? There's something about walking that opens up your primordial will — your animus as the Romans called it. Nietzsche tells us, "All great thoughts are conceived by walking." You hear runners talk about the endorphin rush from running, but no one talks about walking. Walking opens up your mind. It makes the unclear mind clear. It shows you the way.

If you can get out into nature and walk, all the better. When you walk in nature, your primal self will reveal the path. Modernity is a shroud. When I walk, everything becomes clear. I figure out what I have to do. I get inspiration and motivation. Walking reminds me I'm mortal. They say Roman conquerors — when returning to Rome after victory — would have a man follow them during their parade and whisper to them, "You will die." They wanted to be reminded of their mortality, perhaps to stay humble, perhaps to will themselves to greater glory. When I walk, I remember I'm going to die.

I'm compelled to get back home and pursue my great work. Do something that will leave my mark on the world.

Nietzsche had a similar idea to memento mori, which he called the eternal return. He believed that everything in the universe is made of recurring energy. Everything you do in this life will be repeated over and over for the rest of eternity. Imagine the typical American reliving diabetes and all the accompanying complications over and over again for all time. Or the serial masturbator being reborn again and again — just to jack off.

Nietzsche's eternal return is meant to motivate you to pursue the great work, and to say yes to life. You should be devoted to greatness, power, and glory because what you do in this life will be repeated forever. Modernity causes inaction. Whether by our stupidity or nefarious reasons, we've become helplessly inactive. Most days are spent at home looking at a screen. Our jobs are highly specialized requiring little critical thought or satisfaction. There's seemingly no chance for greatness or glory. And you only realize your predicament when you walk — your animus cries out in agony and urges you to FIGHT.

Fight for your future. Fight for your family. Fight for your HONOR. If you take nothing else from what have to say, take this: take walks, venture out into nature, and connect with your primordial will. This alone will show you the path. You may not know what to do or how to break free, but your body does. The fire in your bones will show you the way.

42.
ONE DAY YOU WILL DIE. WHAT DO YOU WANT TO BE REMEMERED FOR?

Everywhere you go, you hear misguided souls talking about equality, social justice, or human rights. These people don't know what they're asking for. They are modern slaves to hidden kings. What they're really asking for is freedom from nature. They don't want to work. They don't want to strive. They simply want an easy, comfortable life. They've convinced theirs is the morally right path and nothing you say or do will convince them otherwise. They're not your frens. Hell, if this was Nazi Germany and you were a Jew, they'd turn you in in a heartbeat.

You must remember you will die. What do you want to be remembered for? The vast majority of men in the West will be remembered for nothing. Their lives are spent in front of screens, working menial jobs. Once their children die, no one will remember they lived at all. That's if they weren't the ignoble end of their bloodline. They're men without any pride or honor. Their bodies are sickly, obese, and frail. At their core, they're cowards — afraid to die. Afraid of sacrifice. They refuse their birthright.

43.
Self-sacrifice always hits a primal chord. It's something women will never understand — because it's not their nature. Men are expendable and every man knows this. So, when you see the ultimate sacrifice, it strikes a chord in your soul. This is why we remember the 300 Spartans at the Hot Gates. Why we remember the Alamo.

The Nazis tried to harness this power of sacrifice in World War II when they abandoned their army at Stalingrad. They told their people back home they were dying to the last man. Only the bastards were still alive — and had to listen to their countrymen talk about them not the radio like they had already died. Nazi Generals redeemed themselves at the end of the war. As the Soviet armies converged on Berlin, they used the last of their forces to draw them away from the city for as long as possible so the women and children could get out. They knew what was happening to women on the frontier at the hands of vengeful Russians.

Ancient men understood sacrifice in the blood. Ancient men would hold the line against impossible odds so that their females and children would have a chance to escape. They would sacrifice themselves to the gods for the goodwill of their tribe. There's an ancient chord that's struck when you see sacrifice, even if it's just in a movie. A good death trumps a long life. The Spartans understood this.

We've forgotten it.

PART VI:

BARBARISM

44.
GREATNESS THROUGH IRRATIONAL SELF-CONFIDENCE

The men we remember, the men who transcend time, whose legends become immortal were men of extreme belief and devotion. These elite men were devoted to — as Ernst Jünger said in *Storm of Steel* — greatness, power, and glory. You must understand that religion is a piece of human nature. Atheism is a religion, even science has become religion. All the low human religions we rail about today are religions for many. What you believe matters. These ideologies may have not started as religions, but humans made them so.

The left often scoffs at Christianity. How can Christians follow their hokey religion and traditions when faced with the "superior" scientific method? If it's not affirmed by the scientific method, it's not real. True believers denounce anything that runs contrary to their religion as heresy. The superior religion — the most intolerant — will win.

The men who turned the wheel of mankind worshipped great men and War Gods. Alexander the Great thought he was descended from Achilles. The Spartans believed themselves descended from Heracles. Mike Tyson believed he was cut from the same cloth as Alexander or Achilles. Some may call such claims delusion and indeed, maybe it was "delusion." But they did become great. What they call delusion was called irrational self-confidence by Heartiste. Cus D'Amato taught it to Tyson through self-affirmations and mindset training. There's great power that comes from irrational self-confidence. Over a long enough time, the irrationally self-confident become true believers in their own worth.

Men must learn about great men and War Gods. Use them as models for greatness. The offer insight into nature and reveal the path forward. The Romans made statues of their heroes, Gods, and ancestors to be reminded up their greatness. To use for motivation. We should do all learn from this.

It's possible many of the great men we remember believed themselves descended from Gods and heroes. Perhaps, their accomplishments confirmed their divine lineage. Perhaps, if you stopped long enough you could hear the War God summoning you to arms. There is an oak tree beside my house. This is a sign. Thor fights by my side. You must look for the influence of the gods in your own life. Also, study great men and heroes. Learn from their legends.

Before his last fight, Tyson said "the Gods of War have summoned me again." They're sending you signs, are you listening?

45.
THE BARBARIAN PRINCIPLE

"The noble caste was always the barbarian caste." -Nietzsche

It's far more important to understand how the world works than any of the new age bullshit the regime is trying to stuff down your throat today. Historically, world powers are often overthrown by rude, barbaric peoples. Barbarians. Everyone by now has seen the meme about how strong men are created.

It's something that's been observed by many throughout history. Teddy Roosevelt said the curse of ancient civilizations was that they were pacified and conquered by some ruder people who had kept their "virile fighting power."

Howard Bloom's *The Lucifer Principle* introduced the same concept. The example he used in the book was the benevolent Persian Empire getting defeated by a band of upstart savages(the Ancient Greks). A great example for today as the Persian Empire also practiced "tolerance and diversity." Nations are built by barbarians.

Empires have varying origin stories and while the Barbarian Principle may not fit all empires, it's happened often enough to be mentioned in the historical record. The Ancient Greks were savages compared to the more civilized Persians. The Romans were founded by a gang who raided nearby villages for their women to continue their civilization. Rome itself was later overran by barbarians after years of decadence and decay. The Barbarian Principle is almost a law of nature and something every people should think about but don't.

The barbarian is closer to nature than the civilized man. He understands what the civilized man never did: nature is brutal. There's no fairness in nature. Nature only cares about who wins. And it is wolves who win wars.

Nature is unforgiving. Those willing to do is what it takes to win will rise to the top. Base your worldview on modern morality at your own peril. Morals aren't bad per se, but the culture that doesn't recognize that it only takes one bad apple to bring it all crashing down. The men who fought in the World Wars were often thought of as the silent generation. They in all likelihood had to do terrible things to win. I don't believe in sheepdogs. In war, it's wolves against wolves.

The wolves who win became the noble caste of the society they create and then, they set it up so power stays in the family. They give themselves the unfair advantage. This happens even in democratic societies. Now — our "noble" caste ain't the same barbarians that created this society. The argument can be made that they're undeserving of their power, but regardless they still have the power and they know how to use it.

Case in point is the eviction moratorium that was issued during the rona virus. These politicians knew it was ending, but somehow didn't get to it until the last day before they left office and voted down the extension. Now millions of Americans will be facing evictions. For the party that ran on "decency," this is low, but expected from the ruling class.

The most important thing you should take away from the Barbarian Principle is this: don't let your fate rest in the hands of the elite. Become elite. Find a way to break the chain. Create your own small tribe and train with your friends. Live on your own terms so when and if the fall happens, you'll be amongst the barbarian caste.

46.
REAWAKEN THE BARBARIC SPIRIT

If you live in America, you should be worried. American men have been completely pacified and disprivileged. They've been taught to believe toxic masculinity is real, the future is female, and that there are some forty other genders. Americans have not yet been defeated at home. They have the massive advantage of being separated from the rest of the world by two oceans. But victory in the Second European Civil War defeated the American spirit. Most "Americans" today believe the greatest threat to the country is white Americans males.

130

American men, however, have already been conquered. You can see it in their eyes and the softness of their bodies. They're being made comfortable and compliant. Rampant mental illness, depression, and obesity are signs that these men know something is wrong in their soul, but the years of social conditioning by "experts" have convinced them all is right. Times will have to get a lot harder for enough Americans to see what I see now, and those hard times may still be a long way off. But if you wait forever the hard times, it may be too late.

Predicting the future is hard, but you can see the direction of the waves. No one can say with accuracy what will happen when, nor is it worth your time. Anything that's happening now however, likely happened before. The answers are in the past. What were the men of powerful civilizations like? What did they do to get there? What did they believe? Figuring that out lays out a course. There was a point where most Americans believed in a concept called the end of history. The devastation of the nuclear age would prevent any serious outbreak of war. But history doesn't end. The clock is still ticking. World powers are still maneuvering against each other while Americans remain blissfully unaware.

Robert E. Howard asked, "*When a nation forgets her skill in war, when her religion becomes a mockery, when the whole nation becomes a nation of money-grabbers, then the wild tribes, the barbarians drive in... Who will our invaders be? From whence will they come?*"

The barbarians are coming. From where is anyone's guess, but if you don't want to get caught with your pants down, you had best become a barbarian first. America may be cracking down on dissent, but it's still a massive country and a massive empire. You've got the room and privacy to make your plans come to life. Americans have forgotten the savage hardness of the colonists who settled in the United States and the frontiersmen who made Manifest Destiny reality. You could not be weak and survive in early America. Life was dangerous and brutal, so too, the American man had to be dangerous and brutal.

The American type that conquered the United States is a type that's echoed throughout history. It was first seen in the Greek tale of Hercules, a Neolithic hunter who ventured out into the chaotic, dark world to defeat chthonic monsters and made the world safe of mankind. The Norse and other early European cultures believed in Thor who shared many similarities to Hercules and his father Zeus. He went out to protect the perimeter, fighting giants and monsters. Hercules and Thor were massive looking with rippling muscled and a savage spiritedness to fight. They inspired countless men throughout time to fight and protect their people from the forces of chaos.

Robert E. Howard's hero Conan the Barbarian is almost the next iteration of this archetype. Howard lived in the aftermath of the frontier and American Civil War. His beliefs came out in his writing and his most popular hero was Conan who was a massive barbarian. Conan is a force of nature. In Howard's works he fights sorcerers, beasts, and simian-like apes. He fights in battles, spends time pirating, and even being on an American-like frontier. He ultimately rises from a lowly thief to capture the country of Aquilonia by strangling the the previous king at the foot of his throne.

When you read the Conan stories, you can get a glimpse of the powerful will to life and power that the Cimmerian possesses. It's a savageness civilized men don't have a concept of. Something Americans need to reawaken in themselves. It's in the blood, your body hasn't forgotten it. You see the same savageness come out when you read about Hercules or Thor. It's a part of being a man. Men were built to go to war. You must find this barbaric spirit again.

47.
BECOME BARBARIAN

The world is a big place. If you try to take it all in, keep up the daily politicsball, you'll at worst blaqpill and at best, get used as a tool by meat grinders. There's no going back to whatever idea you had about America in the past. There's no return to "normalcy." The only way is forward. The system is designed to work like quicksand. The more you try to fight it, it will bury you. Until a figure arises that can bring the leviathan to its knees, you must take on different strategies to win.

Winning is the only thing that matters. Your way of living, your conviction that your right means nothing if you don't win. Nature doesn't care what you believe so long as you win. It's hard to get behind a philosophy like Evola's which suggests you should ride the tiger or surf the Kali Yuga. It feels so passive and resigned to fate, but it doesn't have to be. What I suggest is something similar but different, with a more Nietzschean touch.

What Nietzsche gets right is the idea of man as a beast in nature. He doesn't buy into the bullshit trained to kids today about how enlightened and technologically superior modern man is, how we've effectively become the guardians of nature. It's hubris to believe that garbage.

If you want to know how to go through life, you read Nietzsche. What separates Nietzsche from all other thinkers is he offers paths forward that are easy to understand. Most philosophers use big words to make them seem smart, but they ultimately just convolute their message, or they deal solely in theory. Nietzsche correctly observed culture was degenerating and the cure to culture was a return to the savage. His answer wasn't to just lay down and die. He didn't think we could turn the wheel back. Nietzsche believed man had to be surpassed. One had to become the Overman. This conclusion came from one of his main tenets, the Will to Power. Nietzsche believed everyone — in their blood — had a Will to Power. They wanted to master their conditions and then continue to accumulate more forces and power. To ascend.

Many religions practice a sort of life-denying tendency. Reject this life so you're rewarded later in heaven. Nietzsche believed in saying yes to life. He was life-affirming. And the way to implement this is to realize a truth few would admit, man is a beast in nature. Even in all our "sophistication and technology," you can see glimpses of our animalistic nature if you pay attention.

If a man is a beast in nature, then there are ritualistic actions that got him to the top of the food chain. There is no denying how men have gotten on top. They're first in the pecking order, but this is only contingent on men acting in accordance with nature. The moment they stray too far from the path, nature will sow the seeds of our destruction. It's pertinent then, to study the history of men and figure out how we got to this point. By doing this, you'll isolate the tribes that turned the wheel of mankind forward and be able to learn from their examples.

The most powerful nations and tribes started as barbarians. They were considered primitive to the peoples they overthrew. This is revealing. Savage men conquered superior states because they didn't forget their nature, their virile fighting power, as Teddy Roosevelt called it. Barbarians turn the wheel of mankind. Barbarians aren't stifled by the culture of a rotting society. Barbarians feel the primordial will to power, and they understand natural law: might IS right.

This was a roundabout way of saying you must become barbarian. You must re-barbarize yourself and teach the ways of the barbarian to your sons. No one knows when the current empire will fall, but when it does, the barbarians will come. Best to be among their ranks. The barbarian is life-affirming. He wants to make something of this life. To leave his mark on the world. To whatever extent he has to deal with society, it's not at the cost of his barbarism. The barbarian understands you need a sort of wolffish hardness to survive and thrive in nature.

What a Yes-To-Life mentality does is get your head in the game. You're not going to waste your time dreaming of returning to another time, the only time you have is now. You're not going to out trying to fight a battle you don't even know how to win. The barbarian is going to do the best he can with the time he has. This means accumulating power and finding the means of conquering the conditions he was born into. He's only going to fight the battle he knows he can win. Before that, it's best to fly under the radar, don't turn the eyes of the leviathan onto you until you know you can win.

Some of this philosophy is surfing the Kali Yuga as Evola understands it. The other is taking action to get you and yours closer to victory. The Civil War/Balkanization that everyone wants doesn't seem likely. I'd even argue the American Founding Stock is in no position to win it even if it did occur. Most in this sphere need to focus on building the foundations. Getting stronger. Mastering the martial virtues. Getting detached from the system. Once these conditions are met, the focus will change to accumulating forces, power.

Let's be honest, most men on the right don't look like barbarians. A great deal of them look like dorks. You're not winning any wars with dorks. Dangerous and brutal are the natures of this game. Devotion to these ends, your purpose.

48.
FURY FOR THE BARBARIAN SOUL

This will come off as blaqpill to the uninitiated, but for the barbarians out there, it will be fuel for the fire. There is a distinct movement on the right that is for American greatness — for making America great again — as the most hated god emperor of all time said. This group on the right wants to worship the Founding Fathers, the red, white, and blue, and most importantly, freedom. The America we all thought we lived in. The problem is their beliefs are as much fantasy as the left's ideas about leftism ushering in utopia. America doesn't deserve greatness on any level in its current or past iterations. Now — I'm not taking a pro-leftist talking point.

You need only look at the news cycle to get just a glimpse of how evil the American Empire is. I do not like to use the word evil, I take more of Nietzsche's "Beyond Good and Evil" stance, but the argument for evil can be powerfully made by examining the real America. There are many reasons you should want to see the empire burned to the ground. From events that happened in our age back to the beginning of the country.

Many of the problems of the modern American Empire you will already know and understand. Academia fails consistently in educating its students but does a fine job of creating passive income for its pyramid scheme and leaving its disciples in debt for decades. Academia — which claims to be creating the best minds and bringing progress to America is succeeding only in creating non-player characters. NPCs. People are trained to be manipulated and brainwashed by the system. College gets more expensive every year and the quality of its product reduces in proportion to its price.

It's in our colleges that the crises of mental illness and gender confusion have exploded in recent years. The only history students can seem to remember is freeing the slaves and the holocaust. The institutions that are supposed to be creating great minds are instead making their students sick and demented. But wait — there's more.

Families and traditions are being attacked at every angle by these brainwashed NPCs thinking they're making the world a better place. The war on men was likely the precursor to both gender confusion and transgenders. Along with xenoestrogens, the war on men is helping create men with the testosterone levels of old men along with a host of other mental and physical diseases. The pale face — as James Lafond likes to call the American Founding Stock — is the pinnacle of evil in the modern empire. Yes, the people who make up more than half of the population are the pinnacle of everything wrong with the country. Crimes can be committed against pale faces with impunity because the prosecutors won't prosecute minorities and "allies." Small infractions by pale faces will bring the complete and total power of the American Empire down upon them.

Controlling the people is something every country or state has done since the beginning of time. The first men who did this were primitive astronomers in ancient tribes who figured out the seasons and mystery of the stars. They used this knowledge to convince their fellow cavemen of their superiority. Being able to predict a full moon was power. Later on, the priests took over this role. In today's "sophisticated" society, it falls to the mainstream media. In days past, it was easier, but the internet age made their job extremely difficult. Hell, it blew the top right off. The funniest example of how fake the news is would be weather reporting.

Your favorite news station goes live to a reporter harrowing the violent storm hitting whatever major US city. He's holding on for dear life from the violent winds and rain to bring you the news. And then, in the background, you see a bunch of guys running to the middle of street to do push-ups. Another bit might have a random pedestrian doing cartwheels behind the reporter "braving" the terrible storm. These show just how much credible authority the media has. There is no real journalism or "fact-checking" (another fake industry). Their stories are meant to sensationalize, create outrage, and trigger the well-trained, college-educated into action for some obscure cause.

Now, this does make the media look stupid, but they're very effective at what they do. The media controls the state narrative. It forces the right to speak on whatever they're saying. The media's ability to control the narrative and the news cycle gives them power. They don't need to be credible. They help Americans to have short memories, thus snuffing out any true resistance.

The media have managed to make the President more important than he really is. Sure, he is important, but the power of the American Empire is decentralized. There's no head of the snake you can cut off to achieve victory. You will have to cut off hundreds, if not thousands of heads to even make a mark. And then you have to deal with all the bureaucratic institutions of the US government. There's no real leadership in the empire. Most of the shit you want to complain about was already decided decades before whoever entered the Oval Office. You can't even go after the congressmen or senators. Pelosi's been in office how long? There's no accountability for our "elected representatives" who vote on bills they didn't even read.

Many of these politicians were bought and paid for by corporations and NGOs. Their allegiance is the ones signing the checks which is why the United States would send 400 million dollars to a gender studies program in Pakistan. For the most part, we don't even know who's running the country, and that's by design. They don't want you to know who's responsible. That's a name and a face you can go after. This is why it's better to become rich and anonymous than rich and famous. There's no one for the people to unite against. No one to fight. Their power is decentralized and secure.

49.
BARBARISM IS THE NATURAL STATE OF MAN

If your favorite "masculinity" guru says otherwise, he's trying to sell you something. What does it mean to be a man? It's to be a savage, a barbarian who goes out into the wild to hunt and kill for his tribe and family. The more into civilization you get, the more maternal it becomes. And to become more civilized is to become more emasculated. It's to surrender your manly rites for safety, security, and material. It's living in the way women think you should live. Civilization is the way of women and man has no place in it.

In the primitive tribe, it suited women to be materialistic, to favor words over action. Their job was to stay put. To make noise when danger approaches. To gather material for survival and keep the group unified. The man went out into nature with his friends to protect the tribe from threats and to hunt in order to provide. To survive and thrive in the wild, the man adopted different values from a woman. A woman's values in the wild were liabilities.

Barbarians had to be self-sufficient. They couldn't depend on women to survive. They had to go out into the wild and fight. The hunter needed a different skill set. He had to be quiet to not scare off his prey(recommend reading James Lafond for more insight on this, especially how he recounts situations where he was about to be jumped). They needed strength and power to overcome as well as the conditioning to outlast their prey. They had to embrace the struggle. Embrace the fight for survival. Possess the courage to go out into darkness and face danger.

The way of men is the way of becoming predator. The most important virtue of being a man is not talked about by almost any "guru" who writes about manliness.

A better way to understand a man's purpose is to remove the complications of civilization completely, what did man do in nature? Man was a hunter, the ultimate predator. You must use this to shift to a more manly mindset. "Masculinity gurus" often talk about maxing out certain virtues like strength, courage, and honor. These virtues are important, but they don't make the man. What makes the man is his ability to enter the threshold, to go into the darkness, to hunt and win. You must develop a killer instinct.

The warrior-hunter must take life whether it's a real threat or food. He must look at his enemy's will as something that needs to be broken. It's his will vs another's. My favorite embodiment of this mindset is James Lafond. He spoke on what it's like to be preyed upon by multiple assailants. He knows he's going to lose, but he's resolved to take at least one of them with him to hell. That killer instinct has saved Lafond during his time in "Harm City" as he calls Baltimore. That feeling you get when all you see is red. How can you kill the guy in front of you? The strong silence that takes place, like the Neolithic hunter stalking the lion. Men facing predators with this mentality understand in the blood what they're about to step into. The coward will break, and the man will fight.

Having the killer instinct is the act of imposing your will on your enemies with the intent of breaking their will. You want to break your enemy's spirit. This takes place both mentally and physically. To be a man is to be able to hunt and fight. To play this game of breaking wills. To keep your own will unbroken. And where it does crack, to build it back stronger.

To build this manly instinct to break wills, you have to face adversity. You have to find your limits and push beyond them.

The Greek word Agon from where we get the word "agony" is what they called conflict, the testing of wills. It's the struggle. For men, stress is good. Stress is VITALISM. You have to learn to live in it. To desire the fight and thrive on the struggle. The killer instinct must be forged. The Ancient Romans understood this. They believed each man had an animus, a type of animalistic spirit that a man had to direct towards labor. Ancient Romans wanted to prove the strength of their wills. Their physical power, vigor, and vitality were all directed towards labor in the Herculean sense. These men dwelled on how to direct their animus in a way that would bring them glory. To leave their mark on the world. How do you go about developing the killer instinct? The desire to at the very least go out fighting. To break the wills of your enemies as you fight?

While psychology is the game being played, you must train your physicality to bring it out. The most potent way to do this is to fight. Pick up a martial art like boxing, wrestling, Muay Thai. If financially you're unable to do this, train with your friends. Test your will against other men. Learn to shoot a gun, the modern sword and shield, and train to be a modern warrior. The tamest way to start building this instinct is to powerlift. It's you vs the iron, which gets progressively heavier over time. As you reach your limits, you must go to war with the weight. It becomes an enemy you have to manhandle in order to win.

However you choose to strengthen your will and build the killer instinct, you must remember to condition and condition hard. The legs feed the wolves. When your conditioning fails, the will follows. Do the hard things. Do the things that test your will. Embrace the struggle.

50.

WHAT IS BARBARIC VITALISM?

What is this substack about? What is my HOLY WAR against this disgusting modern world? What is Barbaric Vitalism? It is my purpose to rekindle the fire in men's souls, crush the leftists of this world, and return mankind to the primitive. The leftist — under direction from the regime — refuses to shut up about "progress." These fanatical degenerates believe they can create a liberal paradise free of racism, misogyny, and all the other evil -isms. A world free of the ultimate evil: Whiteness. And they don't see the irony of any of this. They believe the lies of their university education that they are the most educated people in history. Most educated? Doubtful. Most brainwashed? Absolutely.

The best example of their complete brainwashing is this idea of climate change. Of course, there is climate change. It will go through more. They argue that we are responsible for climate change and it's our duty to stop it, to help mankind survive. Yet, look at these preachers of climate change. Remove civilization and they would be dead long before "climate change." What the leftist wants more than anything else is LIBERATION FROM NATURE.

The masters of this world have preyed on the weak-minded and banded them together into an unholy union of the meek. Progress is the word they use to unite them. If the world we live in is the closest to the "progress" they preach about, how come the men of today aren't better than their forefathers? Ok, maybe we're less racist, but if that is your measurement of progress, we're in trouble. I've seen letters from the old America before the Civil War and the people who wrote these letters were more intelligent than most living today. They understood nature and their place in it in a way the progressive will never understand.

What could the frontier American do that our moderns could not? They lived without the comforts of technology. They traveled without vehicles. Had no heating and air. Many knew how to hunt, fight, and cook. They held a powerful understanding of human nature and were not corrupted by progressivism. Throw them out into nature and they had a fighting chance. The barbaric spirit must be reawakened.

This path has one logical conclusion. In some way or another, mankind will be wiped out. Our dependency on technology will be the reason. Progressivism seeks to snuff out the barbaric spirit, the vital fire that took mankind to the top of the food chain. It's possible that no matter what man does, mankind will meet its end, but if you follow the path of re-barbarization, you give yourself a fighting chance. A chance to go down with honor and glory attached to your name. A man must die well.

Most don't think about dying. It's something we know will happen, but somewhere off in the future. Who after all, wants to see themselves in some longhouse attached to ventilator at the end? Resolve to die with dignity and honor. Don't cling to life at the expense of your honor. The way of life for these progressives is massive cope to live without responsibility and cling to life for as long as possible, dignity be damned. And it is their lifestyle that kills them.

This...is not how life was meant to be lived, in some unconscious haze where you parrot liberal platitudes while going out of the way to escape the misery that is the modern condition. This is what entertainment is. It offers you the opportunity to escape this shithole for a short time. Play a game, watch a movie, take a shot. They are means of avoiding your problems and making hard decisions. Almost all of the modern sicknesses come from the refusal to confront the primordial truths of man.

What are these primordial truths? The easiest one to understand is might makes right. The powerful determine right and wrong, regardless of the "truth." World War II is the most recent example of might makes right. The crimes charged against Nazi Germany were committed by all the Allied nations. Soviets holocausted ten million Russians before the war even kicked off. Americans put the Japanese residing in the United States into internment camps. Both sides raped and pillaged the Germans.

The most intolerant always wins. This is not so obvious a truth. The people of peace and diversity would want you to think of this as bullshit. Ask them, however, if they could date someone who was right-wing. How many could? How many could even be friends with or buy from a right winger? How often do these progressives go on tirades about "Whiteness?" Despite all their preaching about inclusion, they are the most intolerant of our time which is why they're winning.

Man is a beast in nature. We as men have forgotten that, we too, are a part of nature. The hubris of man to think that we've risen above this. Nature will decide when it's our time and we don't have a say in this. The best you can do is to live in accordance with nature, with what makes us the ultimate predator. The second mankind lets its status on top of the food chain go to our collective heads is the moment nature sows the seeds of our destruction.

Certain of these primordial truths are found in the blood. They're not easily explained because man is more than just a mental animal. Some of these truths can only be explained through physicality, through action. In action, you can experience what I call Barbaric Vitalism and what Nietzsche called the Will to Power. This primordial will to life that modern man has forgotten must be rekindled or we — and our descendants — will continue to be milked for all we're worth by the greedy powerfucks who rule over us.

Barbaric Vitalism is the conscious decision to listen to what's in the blood, to what our "enlightened progressives" want to snuff out in early childhood. In each of us is a desire to master the conditions we're brought into whereas the liberal-minded would have us settle for the pod and become the ultimate consumer. But this isn't what life is about. Life is about mastering space and leaving your mark on the world. To find purpose in the chaos.

Printed in Great Britain
by Amazon

41971184R00088